science,
marxism and the
big bang

D0921413

science, marxism and the big bang

a critical review of 'reason in revolt'

a contribution to a debate on marxism and science

peter mason

Published by Socialist Publications Ltd

November 2007

Science, Marxism and the Big Bang:
A Critical Review of 'Reason and Revolt'
Peter Mason
© Socialist Publications Ltd 2007

First Edition, November 2007
Second Edition, November 2007

Classification: Peter Mason
Science, Marxism, Dialectics

ISBN 978-1870958-41-7 pbk

A catalogue record for this book is available from the British Library
Published by Socialist Publications Ltd
www.socialistparty.co.uk
Typeset in Utopia 9 pt
Printed by Intypelibra (London)

Distribution by Socialist Books,
PO Box 24697, London, E11 1YD
Telephone +44 (0)20 8988 8789
e-mail: bookshop@socialistparty.org.uk
www.socialistbooks.co.uk

typesetting & design: dennis@kavitagraphics.co.uk

science, marxism and the big bang

a critical review of 'reason in revolt'

a contribution to a debate on marxism and science

peter mason

Acknowledgements

This book was written as a contribution to a debate on Marxism and science. Thanks to all those who read and commented on the manuscript, including Iain Dalton, Ken Douglas, John Edwards, Roy Farrar, Thomas House, Ruth Mason, Sofia Mason, Ronnie Sukdeho, Peter Taaffe, Manny Thain and Peter Van der Biest. Thanks especially to Lynn Walsh for his insightful comments and considerable patience. A special thanks also to Geoff Jones, whose comments on the manuscript, based on a life-long experience of teaching advanced physics, were invaluable. For cover design and layout thanks to Dennis at Kavita Graphics

Peter Mason
November 2007

Introduction

*"Einstein was determined to re-write the laws of physics...
From the standpoint of relativity, steady motion on a straight
line is indistinguishable from being at rest."*
Woods and Grant, Reason in Revolt, 1995

*"First Law of Motion: Every body perseveres in its state of rest, or of
uniform motion in a right line, unless it is compelled to change that
state by forces impressed thereon."*
Isaac Newton, Principia, 1687

Reason in Revolt, *Marxist Philosophy and Modern Science*, written by Ted Grant and Alan Woods (hereafter abbreviated to Woods), attempts a Marxist critique of science.

A Marxist critique of science is a laudable project. But such a critique requires not only an understanding of Marxist theory, but also a thorough comprehension of scientific theories and their historical development. Marxism does not provide a ready-made key for making judgements about scientific ideas. It cannot substitute for a detailed knowledge of the appropriate scientific material. Unfortunately, Woods' analysis, as we will show, reveals a poor understanding of the science he seeks to elucidate.

The past century has seen a transformation of the world through scientific development, whether for good or bad. There has also been a transformation of science itself, many times over, since Karl Marx and Friedrich Engels began the development of what they termed 'scientific socialism', which came to be known as Marxism. Marx and Engels often exchanged correspondence about scientific matters and they were close friends with Carl Schorlemmer, a member of the Royal Society (the UK's national academy of science), who advised them on the latest advances in chemistry.

Engels highlighted the role of scientists in human history. The "immortal work" of Nicolaus Copernicus showed that the earth revolved around the sun. Engels describes its publication as a "revolutionary act". Copernicus "shows theology the door" at the dawn of the Enlightenment, but Isaac Newton closes the period with his "divine first impulse". (*Dialectics of Nature*, Introduction) Engels endorses Immanuel Kant's realisation, at that time unproven, that all "celestial bodies" originated from swirling clouds of gas. Engels calls this conception, "the greatest advance made by astronomy since Copernicus". For the first time, Engels comments, "the conception that nature had no history in time began to be shaken. Until then the celestial bodies were believed to have been always, from the very beginning, in the same states." (*Anti-Dühring*, p72)

Marx and Engels particularly admired Charles Darwin, a revolutionary, iconoclastic scientist in his own modest and hesitant way. Darwin showed how species developed and changed, discovering the secret of life's evolution on our planet. Engels emphasises that "nature does not just exist, but *comes into being* and *passes away*".

One of the cornerstones of scientific socialism is usually termed 'dialectical materialism', although Marx and Engels never used the term themselves. Marx and Engels took the dialectical method of the German philosopher Georg Wilhelm Friedrich Hegel and used it as a tool to understand the historical development of human society, once they had placed his philosophical method on a materialist basis.

In the last century, Marxists debated the revolutionary work of Albert Einstein and the Big Bang theory of the universe, with its origins in the observations of Edwin Hubble. Einstein's theory of relativity and the Big Bang theory combined to overturn every last remnant of the old Newtonian science, which was saturated with the belief in the "absolute immutability of nature", as Engels emphasises. It is these two revolutionary theories, the theory of relativity and the Big Bang, with which the first half of *Reason in Revolt* (first published in 1995) is chiefly concerned.

For this reason our study of the relationship between Marxism and science will focus on the historical development of cosmology and in particular the contribution of Einstein and the Big Bang. We know that our universe exists, but did it come into being and will it pass away?

* * *

"Einstein was determined to re-write the laws of physics," writes Woods. "From the standpoint of relativity, steady motion on a straight line is indistinguishable from being at rest." (p161) But, as we will show, this is not just the standpoint of relativity – it is not a re-write of the laws of physics by Einstein. It is the principle enshrined in Newton's first law of motion. Einstein based his relativity on this law, or more specifically on the *principle of relativity* expounded by Galileo Galilei, dating back four centuries, on which it is based.

After discussing dialectics, Woods moves on to Einstein's theory of relativity, the Big Bang theory, the origin of life, of mind and matter, and other universal matters. Reason in Revolt attempts to discuss 'life, the universe and everything'. The jacket cover asks whether this "encounter" between Marxist philosophy and science will "provide the basis for a new and exciting breakthrough in the methodology of science?"

Woods attempts to make philosophical judgements about scientific ideas based on what he believes to be the dialectical materialism of Marx and Engels. But as Hegel, to whom Woods often appeals in *Reason in Revolt*, wrote nearly two centuries ago, "Truth is concrete". Hegel explains that without a concrete grasp of the subject under study, no clarity can be found. Following Hegel, many other Marxists – Vladimir Lenin in particular – have emphasised that truth is always concrete.

Reason in Revolt's representation of dialectics is rigid and abstract. Lenin's first "element" of dialectics (of which we find no mention in *Reason in Revolt*) is that every thing must be considered "in its relations and in its development". (Lenin, Conspectus of Hegel's Book, *The Science of Logic, Collected Works*, volume 38, pp221-2) By comparison, Woods approaches scientific theories too narrowly, and with insufficient knowledge or consideration of their overall historical development.

Woods tells us: "Decades ago, Ted Grant, using the method of dialectical materialism, showed the unsoundness... of the big bang theory." (p189) Woods argues: "From the standpoint of dialectical materialism, it is arrant nonsense to talk about the 'beginning of time,' or the 'creation of matter'." (pps198-9) Grant and Woods believe that their knowledge of dialectical materialism bestows on them an ability to make decisive judgements on the correctness of science with little need to grapple with the evidence and its scientific interpretations. This is a misunderstanding of dialectical materialism, a misrepresentation of the method of Marx and Engels and of the materialist dialectics they developed.

In our discussion of cosmology, unlike that of Woods, we entertain no illusions that we, as Marxists, have, on the basis of materialist dialectics, ready-made criteria by which we can judge scientific theories. Science is, in any case, always incomplete. The solving of apparent contradictions which perturb scientific theories is the life-blood of scientific endeavour. A minority of scientists do not accept the current theories about the origins of the universe. The Big Bang theory itself began as no more than a curiosity supported by a minority – presenting a solution to Einstein's equations which appeared to fit the observational evidence, but which had little support.

Nevertheless, beginning with the discovery of the cosmic background radiation – the 'fossil evidence' of the Big Bang – in 1965, there has developed a very broad degree of agreement with 'four pillars' of evidence for a hot dense origin to our universe. We intend to demonstrate the historical path along which mainstream science passed until it reached that astonishing cosmological viewpoint – the Big Bang theory of the universe – which Woods incorrectly believes to be incompatible with the philosophy of Marxism. We intend to test Woods' grasp of the subject, his methods, and the criticisms he makes.

*   *   *

R*eason in Revolt* accuses modern physics of a retreat into "mysticism", a "mediaeval view", and is appalled at the "Creation Myth" of the Big Bang theory. Yet it is Woods who retreats to the standpoint of Newton, a standpoint which was overthrown a hundred years ago, as it came increasingly into conflict with scientific experiments. In fact, Newton himself was aware of contradictions in his theories of the universe. He admitted he had no idea, for example, on what basis gravity, his greatest discovery, perpetrated its mysterious instantaneous 'action at a distance' – the effect that binds planets in the vastness of space to their orbits round the sun.

Reason in Revolt claims: "Dialectical materialism conceives of the universe as infinite." (p189) We will attempt to refute this claim. Viewed historically, it was Newton who argued that god is infinite and that therefore space and time must be infinite. Newton was also concerned that his 'universal gravitation' should have caused all the stars in the universe to have attracted each other – they should have all fallen into "one great spherical mass". Newton's solution was to summon the hand of god to set an infinite universe in perfect balance. Newton's infinite universe, as embraced by Woods, is essentially a product of religious ideology. The physicist Brian Greene says: "Experimenters never measure an infinite amount of anything. Dials never spin round to infinity." (*The Fabric of the Cosmos*, p335) Infinity is a key concept in the history of philosophy and science, and anyone serious about the subject must be clear on the issues involved. This is no quibble over terminology but a crucial discussion of ideas.

In the fourth century BCE,[1] the ancient Greek philosopher Aristotle drew a distinction between 'potential' infinity, where, for instance, any number, no matter how big, can always be increased by adding more numbers, and what he called "actual infinity". He pointed out that a potentially infinite series of numbers never reaches actual infinity and, in fact, never leaves the finite. The 'actual' infinite, Aristotle argued, does not exist.

Despite his references to Aristotle, Woods makes no direct mention of this seminal and essentially materialist position. Of course, the study of the concept of infinity has developed over the millennia. But as the physicist Lee Smolin recently wrote, in nature, "we have yet to encounter anything measurable that has an infinite value". Infinities which occur in scientific theories are not likely to be reflecting natural phenomena but errors or limits within the theory itself. Infinites in scientific theories are most likely to be "the way that nature punishes impudent theorists". (Smolin, *The Trouble with Physics*, p5)

Woods takes the opposite view. The universe, he repeats, "as Nicolas of Cusa and others thought, is infinite" (p184) and, "The universe has existed for all time." (p199) Woods claims support from Hegel and Engels but we will show that Woods has turned some of their central views upside down.

Einstein's elegant *general theory of relativity*, published in 1916, solved the mysterious 'action at a distance' of gravity which so puzzled Newton. Einstein showed that gravity and motion are "intimately related to each other and to the geometry of space and time". (Smolin, *The Trouble with Physics*, p4) In 1929, Hubble famously discovered that the universe was rapidly expanding. This strongly inferred that the universe had issued from a hot dense origin and this expansion presented a real solution to Einstein's equations.

In this way twentieth century science removed from cosmology the paradoxes arising from Newtonian notions of infinite time and space. It removed the need for the "divine first impulse". Far from leading to 'creationism', once very tangible evidence of the Big Bang arrived in the form of the discovery of cosmic background radiation, science soon began investigating what we here term the material 'substratum' from which the universe emerged in the Big Bang.

Of course, these new discoveries have not eliminated contradictions from science – there is always a dialectical interplay between theory and data. Our understanding of the universe will continue to advance and change. As we write, particle physicists are nervously awaiting the first results from the Large Hadron Collider, the latest and most powerful particle collider, now expected to be operational in early 2008. Many guess the findings will cause upsets and pose new challenges to the current attempts to unify quantum mechanics and Einstein's general relativity – one of the great unsolved problems of physics.

Yet Woods scorns Einstein's general relativity. He describes it as "mediaeval". Yet, to take one example, the pinpoint accuracy of GPS (Global Positioning System) navigation is achieved by continually recalculating the satellite data using Einstein's equations. Without Einstein's theory, GPS navigation would be less accurate by tens of metres. Woods desires to defend the "fundamental ideas" of Marxism by endorsing the fundamental concepts of the Newtonian universe – in the name of dialectical materialism, moreover. Woods says science has been set back "400 years", yet he wishes to set the clock back to the publication of Newton's *Principia* in 1687.

*   *   *

Woods neither properly represents nor understands the last century of discoveries that have so completely changed the scientific conception of the universe. He misunderstands both dialectical materialism and its approach to science. In his obituary to Ted Grant, Woods claims that *Reason in Revolt* defends "the fundamental ideas of the movement". This review argues that, on the contrary, *Reason in Revolt* misrepresents the fundamental ideas of the movement. Grant, who died in July 2006, undoubtedly contributed much to Marxist thought, but he was not a scientist. With the appearance in the summer of 2007 of a second English edition of *Reason in Revolt* we felt it necessary to attempt to set things to rights. (Page references are to the first edition.) We wish, in the course of this discussion, to defend the genuine ideas of Marxism and suggest that Marxism takes quite a different approach to modern science.

In addition to our scientific survey of the last few centuries of revolutions in cosmology, we will argue that Engels was essentially antagonistic to the idea that our universe is infinite. Almost a hundred years before the Big Bang theory was accepted, Engels discussed both the birth and the death of our universe. We find no mention of this in *Reason in Revolt*. Woods confidently predicts that the infinite universe contains only "galaxies and more galaxies stretching out to infinity". (Preface to the 2001 Spanish edition of *Reason in Revolt*) But Engels refers the reader to Hegel who says that such predictions are merely a "tedious" repetition of known phenomena (in this case galaxies), which never leaves the finite. Support for an infinite universe in this form is a failure of imagination, rather than its triumph.

For two-and-a-half millennia, many philosophers have supported the view that infinity is an imaginary concept which has no actual existence. Hegel arrived at a dialectical proposition which can be expressed like this: you can always imagine an unending series of galaxies following one after another, but in concrete reality, at a certain point, quantity turns into quality and a new phenomenon emerges. Whatever existed before is negated. From this point of view there may be many galaxies undiscovered, or many universes beyond our own – it is speculation – but at some point, some other property will arise that ends the tedious repetition, whether of galaxies or universes, the conception of which is beyond our current scientific horizons.

A comment on the preface to the second English edition of *Reason in Revolt*

n May 2007 the publication of a second English edition of Reason in Revolt was announced. In the Preface to the new edition, Woods tells us that when Ted Grant and he were writing *Reason in Revolt* in 1995:

> *"… we were still unsure about the existence of black holes."*
> Preface to the second edition of *Reason in Revolt*

Ted Grant was scathing about the science of black holes, at least until 1990. While *Reason in Revolt* takes a more equivocal stance in part, Woods was certain, in 1995, that the modern physics of the black hole was quite wrong. Woods says:

> *"Singularities, black holes where time stands still, multiverses…*
> *These senseless and arbitrary speculations are the best proof that*
> *the theoretical framework of modern physics is in need of*
> *a complete overhaul."*
> *Reason in Revolt*, p174

Now Woods appears to unreservedly embrace the science of "black holes where time stands still". In the 2007 preface to the second edition he states:

> *"They are present at the centre of every galaxy and serve to hold*
> *galaxies together, giving them the cohesion without which life, and*
> *ourselves, would be impossible. Thus, what appeared to be the most*
> *destructive force in the universe turns out to have colossal creative*
> *powers. The dialectical conception of the unity of opposites thus*
> *received powerful confirmation from a most unexpected source!"*
> Preface to the second edition of *Reason in Revolt*

Yet black holes are not proven. They "remain largely theoretical" and even problematic, as the *New Scientist* pointed out its recent cover story, 'The

Truth About Black Holes'. (6 October 2007) Woods' original scathing condemnation of the modern science of black holes has been replaced by a contrary position which just as surely misrepresents modern science. Black holes are not by any means known to be – or even generally regarded to be – at the centre of "every" galaxy. Black holes are thought to be at the centre of a certain type of galaxy (including our own), at least in most cases, according to a study which Woods came across and misreports in the preface to the 2001 Spanish edition of *Reason in Revolt*.

Reason in Revolt reaches the pinnacle of its ridicule of modern science in its condemnation of the modern science of black holes and the Big Bang theory. Yet there is no direct mention of this in the 2007 preface. Instead, Woods comments on the correct method by which to apply dialectical materialism. Woods quotes Engels, who criticises the idealism of Hegel. Engels says:

> *"The mistake lies in the fact that [the laws of dialectics] are foisted on nature and history as laws of thought, and not deduced from them."*
>
> *Dialectics of Nature*, Chapter 2

Does not Woods make the same type of mistake? Does not Woods attempt to foist on cosmology what he believes are the laws of dialectical materialism? Reviewing, with complete incomprehension, the modern science of the Big Bang in relation to Einstein's general theory of relativity, Woods cries, "Here the study of philosophy becomes indispensable." (p216) *Reason in Revolt* tells us that science has regressed to:

> *"...the world of the Creation Myth (the 'Big bang'), complete with its inseparable companion, the Day of the final Judgement (the 'big crunch')."*
>
> *Reason in Revolt*, p183

Yet only seven years later, in the 2002 USA edition of *Reason in Revolt*, Woods offers his support to a mainstream re-working of the old speculative cyclical Big Bang theory, complete with its infinite Big Bangs and Big Crunches.

1 BCE – "Before the Common Era", a secular alternative term for BC, "Before Christ"

Science and dialectics in *Reason in Revolt*

Phase changes, or the transformation of quantity into quality and vice versa

Reason in Revolt sets out to explain the laws of dialectics using modern scientific examples. In the section, *Quantity and Quality*, Woods discusses the dialectical concept of the transformation of quantity into quality, which is exemplified, as we shall see, by the way heated water changes into steam. This is an important concept both for Marxists and also for scientists, who use the term 'phase change' or 'phase transition' for changes such as the transition from a liquid to a gaseous state.

Georg Wilhelm Freidrich Hegel (1770-1831)

In modern philosophy, the concept was first fully developed by Hegel, who took it from the ancient Greeks.

Hegel used the example of water changing from a liquid to a gas in his *Science of Logic* and elsewhere. He showed how a constant addition of a quantity of heat to water leads to a 'qualitative leap' at boiling point. Water above boiling point no longer has the 'quality' of being a liquid. Instead, it is a gas, a qualitatively different form of matter.

Criticising the maxim, 'Nature does not make leaps', Hegel wrote:

> "*Again, water when its temperature is altered, does not merely get more or less hot but passes through from the liquid into either the solid or gaseous states; these states do not appear gradually; on the contrary, each new state appears as a leap, suddenly interrupting and checking the gradual succession of temperature changes at these points.*"
>
> *Science of Logic*, p369

Additional quantities of heat at boiling point do not lead (under normal circumstances) to a further increase in the temperature of the water, it leads to a qualitative change – water turns from a liquid into a gas. The same applies if the temperature of water is reduced:

"Water, in cooling, does not gradually harden as if it thickened like porridge, gradually solidifying until it reaches the consistency of ice; it suddenly solidifies, all at once. It can remain quite fluid even at freezing point if it is standing undisturbed, and then a slight shock will bring it into the solid state."

Science of Logic, p370

Hegel's observations are scientifically accurate. Physicists call this type of change, when water changes from a liquid phase to a gaseous phase, a phase change. The fact that nature makes leaps from one form to another, such as from a liquid to a gas, is seen as an important concept in physics and cosmology today. Brian Greene explains how cosmologists today examine periods in the distant past when the rapidly expanding early cosmos itself underwent phase changes (speculation about a period of "inflation" in the early universe is thought to undergo phase changes). Greene himself uses the example of water changing into a gas. The concept of phase changes or transitions, Greene comments, "helped scientists make definite predictions that have been experimentally proved". (*The Fabric of the Cosmos*, p268)

This process of change is represented in materialist dialectics in the expression, "the transformation of quantity into quality and vice versa". The addition of "vice versa" indicates that the reverse is true: a change of quality brings new characteristics which can be quantitatively measured. For instance, the qualitative change of water from a liquid to a gas brings about a gas with a certain pressure and temperature which can be quantified.

In discussing the maxim, 'Nature does not make leaps', Hegel was also seeking a justification for leaps that take place in society – revolutions. Hegel is well aware that the French Revolution of 1789 was described as "unnatural" by detractors such as Edmund Burke, the 'father of Conservatism'. Burke argued that unless change is gradual it will end in disaster because nature does not make leaps.

Woods also attempts some scientific observations while giving the same example of the phase changes of water. But unlike Hegel and Engels, his scientific knowledge is lacking. For instance, he states:

"Until it reaches boiling point, the water keeps its volume. It remains water, because of the attraction of the molecules to one another."

Reason in Revolt, p49

But water does not "keep its volume" and neither Hegel nor Engels suggest that it does. If a liquid is heated it expands and its volume increases: this is how a thermometer works. Further, it "remains water" even when it turns to a gas (water vapour or steam). And it does not remain liquid because of the "attraction of the molecules to one another" but because of atmospheric pressure. Lower the atmospheric pressure sufficiently and the water will boil without any addition of heat.

Woods then states that the volume between the atoms increases in water which is heated which, of course, must mean an increase of the volume of the water as a whole. He then attempts to describe boiling at the molecular level. He writes:

> "*However, the steady change in temperature has the effect of increasing the motion of the molecules. The volume between the atoms is gradually increased, to the point where the force of attraction is insufficient to hold the molecules together.*"
>
> *Reason in Revolt*, p49

But Woods has confused melting with boiling. In *Dialectics of Nature*, Engels discusses phase changes at the molecular level in great detail, but makes no such scientific errors (relative to his epoch, of course).

Melting takes place during the heating of a solid, such as ice, when the molecules become too energetic and the bonds between them break. This is what Woods' description resembles. In this way ice turns into water, which flows with little restriction from molecular bonds. Boiling essentially takes place when, during heating, evaporating molecules become more and more numerous until, at a certain point, these molecules escaping from the surface of the water counteract the pressure of the air molecules on the surface of the water. At this point the water boils. It is quite a different process. This is standard science which can be found in any textbook.

In *Dialectics of Nature*, Engels quotes Hegel on the phase change of water, and then goes on to give a very significant example:

> "*Similarly, a definite minimum current strength is required to cause the platinum wire of an electric incandescent lamp to glow; every metal has its temperature of incandescence…*"
>
> *Dialectics of Nature*, p87

This particular type of leap in nature, the points at which metals glow at various specific stages of heating, (e.g. red hot, white hot, etc) was vexing the minds of the scientists of the time. They were looking for an equation which showed how gradual processes could lead to these sudden changes in colour, or different energy states. But none seemed to work. When, at the turn of the 20th century, Max Planck found a formula which satisfied experimental observation, the formula contained discrete leaps from one energy level to another. Planck termed the discrete packets of energy, suggested by his formula, "quanta".

Had they been alive to witness it, Marx and Engels would have derived no small satisfaction at Planck's discovery, not least because Hegel, discussing leaps in nature, quite coincidentally even used the same term. Any existing thing, Hegel wrote, "is essentially a relation of quanta". This quanta may undergo "quantitative alteration", Hegel continues, within a range in which it "does not change its quality". But, "there enters a point in this quantitative alteration at which the quality is changed and the quantum shows itself ... so that the altered quantitative relation is converted into ... a new quality, a new something." (*Science of Logic*, p367) Planck's quanta marked the beginning of quantum mechanics, which takes for its basis that physical systems (such as atoms) leap from one discrete energy state to another.

Electrons and protons

In another discussion of dialectics in the section, *The Unity and Interpenetration of Opposites*, Woods aptly uses the atom as an example of how opposites interact with each other.

In an atom, electrons swarm round a nucleus composed of protons and neutrons. But the electrons carry the opposite charge to the protons, and in this way, among many others, all physical things made of atoms are comprised of, or are "interpenetrated" by, opposites. Woods quotes Richard Feynman, the US physicist, who said "All things, even ourselves, are made of fine-grained, enormously strongly reacting plus and minus parts, all neatly balanced out." (Feynman quoted in *Reason in Revolt*, p64)

The opposite charges are united in the atom. In capitalist society, the 'opposites' of the exploiting boss and exploited worker are also bound together and mutually dependent in the production process. Opposing classes are united (in a geographical sense) in each capitalist county. They are a unity of opposing forces in this sense. But these opposing forces will lead, under the right conditions, to an explosion.

After reading Hegel's *Science of Logic*, Lenin regarded this concept of a unity of opposites as central to dialectics. Lenin quotes Hegel, who said that the understanding of "opposites in their unity" is "the most important aspect of dialectic". (*Science of Logic*, p56) We will discuss the origins of this concept in ancient Greece shortly, where it can be traced to the Ionian philosophy of 'coming into being' and 'passing away', and we will meet it again when we discuss the nature of modern science.

But Woods' science is weak. Pointing out that the electron has a negative charge and the proton a positive charge, Woods begins by asking:

> "*Why do the contradictory forces of electrons and protons not cancel each other out? Why do atoms not merely fly apart? The current explanation refers to the "strong force" which holds atoms together.*" *(p64)*

But the contradictory 'forces' of electrons and protons do cancel each other out, in the sense that the atom becomes neutrally charged if it has the same number of electrons and protons.

The striking thing is not that electrons and protons do not 'cancel each other out' but that they do. The proton has 1836 times the mass of the electron, but exactly the same size charge, only positive rather than negative. The question 'why do atoms not fly apart' seems like an odd question to ask also. After all, the positive and negative charges of the electron and proton attract each other. And what puzzled scientists, before the development of the science of quantum mechanics, was why the electron did not spiral into the atom's nucleus. The strong force, incidentally, does not hold the electrons and protons together as Woods appears, perhaps unintentionally, to state (elsewhere he gets this right), the electrical force does.

Woods gives a number of examples of opposites, but then concludes with a rather sweeping statement:

> "*There are two kinds of matter, which can be called positive and negative. Like kinds repel and unlike attracts.*" *(p65)*

This curious statement (two kinds of matter?) is reminiscent of the outlook of the German idealist philosopher Friedrich Schelling at the turn of the 19th Century. Schelling used the example of the north and south poles of the magnet as a metaphor for the world and its contents, to suggest that change in nature expresses itself through a duality of polar opposites, a philosophy that was very influential for a period. In this way, Schelling, for a period a close friend of Hegel, contributed to the development of the dialectic of the interpenetration of opposites, which Hegel developed further.

But Woods' statement reduces the complexity of the universe and its contents to a very crude formulation. What of gravity, of the neutron, of quarks and neutrinos and those sub-atomic particles which appear to come in sets of threes in various ways? The dialectic of the interpenetration of opposites is a tool which in various ways can undoubtedly aid the comprehension of nature and society, but it is reduced to an absurdity in such sweeping pseudo-scientific statements which can lead to objections or even ridicule from the scientifically minded.

Everything flows

The first passage on modern science in *Reason in Revolt* comes at the beginning of the section, *Everything Flows*. Woods claims:

> *"Particles are constantly changing into their opposite, so that it is impossible even to assert their identity at any given moment. Neutrons change into protons, and protons into neutrons in a ceaseless exchange of identity." (p45)*

There is no truth in this. A neutron that has escaped from an atomic nucleus will decay after about twelve minutes into three particles: a proton, an electron and a neutrino, but this process is quite different to the "ceaseless exchange" pictured here. Later, Woods says that the famous German physicist Werner Heisenberg's exchange force "implied" this supposed "ceaseless exchange" of identity between protons and neutrons. (p96) It does not. The exchange force deals with exchanges between identical particles, not different ones, which would lead to a violation of the law of conservation of charge. It is a well-understood phenomenon.

Although dialectics certainly suggests that science will find a time limit beyond which protons will decay in some way, and teams of scientists are testing to find that limit – nevertheless the proton is stable over very long periods. A twelve-year experiment, started in 1989, suggested that the proton has a lifetime of at least ten million billion billion billion years (10^{34} years – ten with 34 zeros after it). It does not ceaselessly change, as Woods asserts.

Woods' aim is to suggest that nature is not immutable but that change penetrates down to the most fundamental particles. In many ways this is true, if one avoids sweeping statements. But what Woods applies to the smallest particles he will not apply on the largest scale. Engels showed that in the Newtonian conception of the universe, "nature was obviously in constant motion, but this motion appeared as an incessant repetition of the same processes", and thus nature was seen as essentially immutable. Kant, says Engels, changed all that. (*Anti-Dühring*, p73) Yet, surely, when Woods concludes his discussion of cosmology and modern physics he retreats to the point of view of this same "incessant repetition of the same processes". He writes: "All individuals must perish, but the wonderful diversity of the material universe in all its myriad manifestations is eternal and indestructible. Life arises, passes away, and arises again and again. Thus it has been. Thus it will ever be." (p225)

A fundamental law of dialectics: truth is concrete

Woods is no scientist – he has no grounding in science at all. Explaining the energy contained in a gram of mass, Woods gives the answer measured in ergs, an obsolete unit of energy universally replaced by the Joule in 1960. Science has accumulated many observations and has considerably changed in the near half-century since 1960 – some theories considered by scientists to be highly speculative in 1960 are now robustly proven, while others have long since been abandoned.

Woods approaches science as a philosopher of dialectical materialism. He claims that *Reason in Revolt* has had a "tremendous success internationally". But it has had no impact whatsoever on science, undoubtedly for the reasons shown above.

Many readers of *Reason in Revolt* were no doubt attracted by the promise of an exposition of the philosophy of dialectical materialism and its relationship to science, or the development of an understanding of the world we live in – for instance, whether our universe has a definite origin in time and space, or is infinite. We will shortly discuss what the proponents of dialectics, from ancient Greece to modern times, said about these ideas, and discuss the relationship of these ideas to the development of science. It is indeed a fascinating subject.

But by disregarding the need for a thorough understanding of science – as if philosophy can substitute for a detailed understanding of the matter being studied – Woods does an immediate disservice to dialectics and, thereby, to Marxism. Woods forgets that Hegel himself sets out, from the outset, an important law: truth is concrete.

At the start of his *Encyclopaedia*, for example, Hegel says:

> "*Everybody allows that to know any other science you must have first studied it, and that you can only claim to express a judgement upon it in virtue of such knowledge. Everybody allows that to make a shoe you must have learned and practised the craft of the shoemaker, though every man has a model in his own foot, and possesses in his hands the natural endowments for the operations required. For philosophy alone,*

it seems to be imagined, such study, care, and application are not in the least requisite."

Encyclopaedia, paragraph 5

Nikolai Chernyshevsky said Hegel's dialectical method insists that:

"Every object, every phenomenon has its own significance, and it must be judged according to the circumstances, the environment, in which it exists. This rule was expressed by the formula: 'there is no abstract truth; truth is concrete.'"

Chernyshevsky, quoted by Georgi Plekhanov in
The Development of the Monist View of History, pp103-4

Woods should be left in no doubt whatsoever about the importance of this principle of dialectics. Lenin echoes Chernyshevsky: "One of the basic principles of dialectics is that there is no such thing as abstract truth, truth is always concrete." (*One Step Forward, Two Steps Back,* last chapter)

Leon Trotsky says this about dialectics and science:

"Dialectics and materialism are the basic elements in the Marxist cognition of the world. But this does not mean at all that they can be applied to any sphere of knowledge, like an ever-ready master key. Dialectics cannot be imposed upon facts; it has to be deduced from facts, from their nature and development... You will get nowhere with sweeping criticisms or bald commands."

Problems of Everyday Life, p 288

How can Woods construct a dialectical criticism of modern science when he does not understand how water boils? And how will he fare with Einstein's theory of relativity? We will come to this later.

Concepts of the universe – an historical survey

One of the major themes running throughout *Reason in Revolt* is the infinite. Woods repeats many times, claiming the support of dialectical materialism, that the universe is infinite in space and time: "Dialectical materialism conceives of the universe as infinite." (p189)

"From the standpoint of dialectical materialism," Woods intones, it is "arrant nonsense" to talk about the beginning of time or the creation of matter:

> *"Time, space and motion are the mode of existence of matter, which can neither be created nor destroyed. The universe has existed for all time."* (pp198-9)

Is it true that dialectical materialism conceives of the universe as infinite in time and space? Is it a materialist claim? Is it a dialectical claim?

The view that the universe is infinite in time and space may strike many people as a perfectly natural one. This concept has developed over the last five hundred years and should be understood in its historical development. It is a view that arises from definite historical and social conditions.

The Big Bang theory may well seem contrary to common sense to many readers. If we start from the very beginning – with the ancient Greek philosophers from whom so much has been learnt, even by modern scientists – we will find the answer to why science has taken this plunge into what appears on the surface to be an assertion that something can come out of 'nothing': that the universe – all its matter and energy, time and space – can emerge from the Big Bang. We will also discover the real material basis on which science establishes the origins of our universe, and the ancient dialectical concepts which proved so perceptive.

But first, a few remarks on what is meant by 'universe' and 'infinity'.

One universe or many?

irstly, what does Woods mean by the 'universe'? When we say "the world" we may mean one of two things. We may mean the entire universe, or we may be referring to the earth. But what precisely do we mean by the 'entire universe'? No one imagined galaxies beyond our own, let alone universes, until a remarkable eighteenth century German philosopher suggested that there were other "island universes".

This philosopher was Immanuel Kant, who was later to reintroduce the ancient Greek concept of dialectics into modern philosophy. In the late nineteenth century Engels enthusiastically praised Kant's foresight and, in time, island universes were discovered by powerful telescopes, and termed 'galaxies'. By the 1920s, the very great distances of some of these galaxies from our own galaxy had been measured.

Immanuel Kant (1724-1804), son of a German craftsman, introduced dialectics into modern philosophy

After Einstein overturned Newtonian physics and especially with the advent of the Big Bang theory of the origins of the universe, it became possible to conceive of universes outside of our own, leading to various concepts of a *multiverse* or *meta-universe* – a set of universes which are speculated to arise in various ways. So now, when we say 'the universe' we may not mean everything that exists, but only 'our universe' as opposed to possible other universes. To most physicists the term 'the universe' tends to refer to our universe, the universe we can observe. The Astronomer Royal, Martin Rees, who adopts the term "our universe" in this way, writes:

"What's conventionally called 'the universe' could be just one member of an ensemble. Countless others may exist in which the laws [of physics] are different..."

"This new concept is, potentially, as drastic an enlargement of our cosmic perspective as the shift from pre-Copernican ideas to the realisation that the Earth is orbiting a typical star on the edge of the Milky Way, itself just one galaxy among countless others..."

"The big bang that triggered our entire universe is, in this grander perspective, an infinitesimal part of an elaborate structure that extends far beyond the range of any telescope."

Rees, *Before the Beginning, Our universe and others*, p3-4)

Our universe appears to have had a hot, dense origin popularly known as the Big Bang. It does not exclude the possibility of other universes beyond our own. Scientists speculate about a substratum, as we term it here, from which universes might naturally arise. For instance, some envisage universes budding off from a quantum substratum like bubbles budding off from foam. But in modern science neither our universe, nor a multiverse consisting of many universes, is compatible with the old Newtonian universe defended by Woods.

For many scientists today, one significant element of our universe is the special physical attributes of atomic particles and forces of which it is comprised: "The entire physical world," says Rees, referring to our universe, "is essentially determined by a few basic 'constants': the masses of some so-called elementary particles, the strength of the forces – electric, nuclear and gravitational – that bind them together and govern their motions." (Rees, *Before the Beginning*, p236)

But if these forces were only marginally different the universe that we know would be a physical impossibility. Yet we do not know whether these forces are the only possible combination of constants – maybe there are many other possible variations, producing many other types of universe, beyond our own, which are hardly conceivable to us today.

In our universe the known physical laws appear to apply universally, and the space, time, matter and energy of our universe are bound together. Scientists often use the term space-time, meaning, in a special sense, that time and space together can be treated as a single phenomenon. This discovery was based on Einstein's theory of relatively, which also showed that mass and energy are linked. For instance, when an atomic bomb explodes a small amount of enriched uranium is converted into a massive amount of energy, a dreadful demonstration of the truth of Einstein's theory.

In Newton's universe, space and time have an absolute existence of their own, independent of each other and of matter. Einstein showed that if the mass of our universe exceeded a certain amount, the gravity of the universe would cause space-time to bend until the universe became 'closed' like a sphere (which has three dimensions), but in the four dimensions of space-time (which is not easily conceived by us). By closed, we roughly mean that anyone travelling in the universe in what appears to be a straight line could eventually find themselves back at their starting point, as if we were ants scurrying around the inside wall of a gigantic football.

Diagram 1: Space is bent around a massive object such as a star

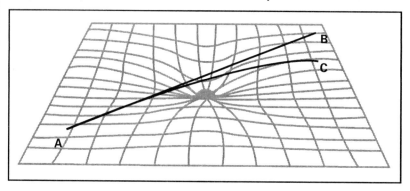

The star is shown by the dimple. To an observer from a distance, distances have been shortened, and time is also running a little slower. Light (shown by the A-C line) passing nearby is bent from the straight path indicated by the the A-B line.

We will discuss how Einstein revolutionised our concepts of time and space in the course of this survey. But to anticipate these arguments slightly, let us take a moment to consider what this remarkable concept means. A star, like our sun, bends space and time – something that has been routinely confirmed by observation since 1919.

Light travelling to earth from a star will be bent if it passes close to an intermediate star or galaxy. Space and time are bent by the great mass of this intermediate star or galaxy, and light passing through this bent space and time behaves just as if it was going though a gigantic lens. Today, this is routinely observed and quantified. It can give rise to gravitational lensing, an extremely useful tool in astronomy, in which a galaxy or other object in front of a distant object acts like a giant magnifying glass.

In the same way, the mass of all the stars in the universe collectively, together with other matter, have the effect of bending the space and time of the entire universe – and if there is enough mass, it could be bent right round back on itself in various ways. Current observations, however, suggest that there is not enough mass for this to happen.

We should point out that Woods calls this result of Einstein's general theory of relativity a "regression to the mediaeval world outlook of a finite universe", in a short passage particularly densely populated with false ideas. (pp382-3) But we should also point out that earlier in *Reason in*

Revolt, Woods has already unintentionally endorsed the idea of space-time bending, not once but twice: "This was proved in 1919, when it was shown that light bends under the force of gravity." (p106) Later, Woods presents both his viewpoints on the same page, first appearing to deny or at least denigrate Einstein's theory and then going on to say that:

> "... [Einstein] predicted that a gravitational field would bend light rays...
> In 1919... Einstein's brilliant theory was demonstrated in practice."
> (p154)

Woods seems to fail to grasp here that the 1919 experiment attempted to show that space and time are distorted by the existence of a massive body and that the effect of gravity is a consequence of this distortion. Arthur Eddington's famous 1919 observations, taken during an eclipse on the island of Principe off the West African coast, showed that light from a star that passed very close to the sun was indeed bent by the mass of the sun.

Eddington's grand expedition was the first experimental test of Einstein's general theory of relativity. His measurements were soon improved upon, and much more accurate measurements have confirmed his result – the confirmation of Einstein's prediction that space and time is warped. Newton's theory of gravity can also be used to suggest that light bends by a certain amount. But Einstein's theory predicts that the gravitational effect on light should cause it to bend by roughly twice as much as predicted by Newtonian science – and light does, indeed, bend by the amount predicted by the general theory of relativity as it follows the curvature of space-time.

When scientists today speculate about other 'island universes' they may envisage universes governed by different laws which lie beyond the space-time of our universe and which, therefore, could not be measured in distances and times from our universe. Such universes might not be gravitationally attracted to one another or to the matter in our universe and may have none of the basic 'constants' as Rees calls them, of our universe – or even, some suggest, the same space-time dimensions. Science stands on the very first stepping-stone of a path to the possible discovery of other universes, in the same way that Kant anticipated a vast enlargement of our horizons when he speculated about other 'island universes'.

So the term 'the universe' today can either refer specifically to our universe or, more broadly, to our universe and anything that may lie beyond it. But Woods is defending the old Newtonian notion of an essentially unchanging universe comprised of infinite time and space with "galaxies and more galaxies stretching out to infinity".

What is infinity?

What does Woods mean by infinity? In the section, *Does the Infinite Exist?* Woods suggests that:

"The idea of the infinite seems difficult to grasp, because, at first sight, it is beyond all human experience." (p353)

An infinite universe would indeed be "beyond all human experience". As the physicist Brian Greene says: "Experimenters never measure an infinite amount of anything. Dials never spin round to infinity. Meters never reach infinity. Calculators never register infinity." (*The Fabric of the Cosmos*, p335)

But this raises precisely the question we will address in this survey: how did the universe come to be reckoned to be infinite?

After all, science, which is instinctively materialist, bases itself on human experience (including, of course, through the use of scientific instruments of all kinds), not on what is "beyond all human experience". This raises a second question: how can Woods' claim that the universe is infinite be a materialist claim?

We can all envisage an unending series of numbers, a series of numbers that continually grows greater in an infinite repetition of some additional amount. No matter how large the number gets, we can always add one more. A simple repetitive task, we imagine, at least in principle, can always be repeated in an infinite process that need never stop. In this sense, we cannot agree with Woods' claim that the infinite seems "difficult to grasp".

But it is important to realise that this infinite process of addition or repetition will never reach actual infinity. The number of repetitions, however large, will be a finite number, and will remain finite.

This infinite process is not the kind of infinity that Woods is talking about. "Infinity, by its very nature cannot be counted or measured." (p353) "The idea of infinity cannot begin with one, or any other number. Infinity is not a mathematical concept." (p218)

Potential and actual infinity

So we begin to see that, contrary to Woods' assumption, there are two contrasting concepts of infinity which may concern us here. (We will glance at George Cantor's contribution to this subject later.) The first is the familiar one, which can, in fact, begin with one, or any other number, where we can always imagine adding one more in an infinite process.

Woods does not accept this, but this is what Aristotle, the Greek philosopher of the fourth century BCE, termed "potential" infinity. It is a process that never leaves the finite – you never reach infinity – yet, at any particular stage under consideration, it is an infinite process. It is the only type of infinity which science recognises (in the real world, as opposed to mathematical methods such as calculus). The dial never reaches infinity even if the process appears to be infinite.

In this way, as we shall see later, Engels at one point envisaged a universe rolling out indefinitely in time and space, in an infinite process comprised only of finites, and never becoming infinite (*Anti-Dühring*, Part V, p67). Elsewhere, Engels envisaged the death of the universe, pointing out that at a certain point all the stars must exhaust their fuels.

The second concept of infinity – the only one that Woods recognises – is "beyond all human experience". Aristotle calls this second type of infinity "actual infinity". Woods claims that the infinite is quite distinct from the finite. Yet Aristotle and many philosophers and scientists, through the ages to the present day, have explained that the 'actual infinite', the infinite that is "beyond all human experience" according to Woods, is an ideal with 'potential' but no 'actual' reality.

Engels' views

Before we start our historical survey let us address directly the question: is the universe – or for that matter, the 'multiverse' – infinite?

We answer this question in the course of this discussion, but to jump ahead, it may be useful to take a glimpse at Engels' remarkable insight on this question. We will argue that among Engels' insights, guided by dialectical considerations, are some that approximate to the position of modern science today.

As we will show, Engels discusses the coming into being of our universe and says that there must have been a cause to this event even if, at present, we have no idea what it is. In today's terminology, science assumes that there must be a cause to the Big Bang and is searching for it.

But if one was to ask whether there must be an infinity of previous causes to the cause of the Big Bang, at another point Engels replies: infinity is a contradiction, and is full of contradictions (*Anti-Dühring*, PartV, p66). Engels was well

Friedrich Engels (1820-1895)

aware that Aristotle had shown that the actual infinite does not exist. It was common knowledge. It was also common knowledge that Aristotle discovered contradictions in the concept of actual infinity, and others, beginning with Galileo, have discovered many more. One such contradiction is called the *infinite replication paradox*, and simply follows from the fact that infinity can contain within it an infinite number of infinities.

Consider an infinity of people. With more than six billion people in the world, there are bound to be people who look very much like you. Famous people sometimes employ look-alikes to pretend to be them. Since antiquity it was understood that if the universe was infinite – a Newtonian universe or a multiverse of modern conception – there must be an infinite number of worlds (or universes) of every possible type, since even the most improbable worlds occur infinitely given an eternity of time and an infinity of space. Among them there will be an infinite number of worlds like ours, and even an infinite number of people like us living on these worlds – in fact, there must be an infinite number of people exactly like us, on these infinite worlds, doing exactly what you and I are doing right now.

As materialists, we must leave the actual infinite for what it is, a contradiction. As scientists emphasise, we have no material evidence for an infinite universe – just a sense that there must always be an endless chain of causes. Let us now place our discussion in its proper historical context.

The dialectic of *becoming* in ancient Greece

Woods seeks to enlist two ancient Greek philosophers in his scheme of the infinite, so this historical survey must begin with them. These two philosophers are Anaximander, from the sixth century BCE, and Aristotle, from the fourth century BCE.

Anaximander – the dawn of dialectics

Both materialism and dialectical thought can be traced back to the sixth century BCE and a remarkable and powerful city-state called Miletus, in Ionia (now Turkey).

In those days Miletus was experiencing a period of revolutionary upheavals as a rising merchant class challenged the old ruling elite for power. These revolutionary upheavals must have been earth shattering, like the 1789 French revolution (in which King Louis XVI was guillotined), or the 1917 Russian revolution. In those revolutions the whole social order was turned upside down – everything in the social order which seemed eternal was proved to be ephemeral, like the so-called 'divine right of kings'. Something similar happened in Miletus. The rising merchant class for a time took power from the old aristocracy in a series of revolutions.

This revolutionary period gave birth to the philosophy of dialectics. It is no coincidence that Kant and Hegel, who made dialectics central to their philosophy and greatly developed the ancient dialectics founded in Miletus, also lived in such revolutionary times – the period of the 1789 French revolution. It was in these momentous events, as one class clashed with another, that these philosophers came to believe that a clash of opposites leading to a sudden qualitative, fundamental change represented the true underlying nature of all things.

In ancient Ionia, this brought about the philosophical school thought to have been founded by Thales and Anaximander, and it is called the Ionian school of philoso-

Anaximander (610-547 BCE)

phy. It will hopefully become clear that our discussion of this ancient philosophy is very relevant to the claims made in *Reason in Revolt* about dialectical materialism and the universe.

No doubt reflecting the revolutionary times in Miletus, in which it must have seemed that nothing was permanent, Anaximander speculated that the entire universe had come into being from some unknown substratum and would eventually perish.

Woods says, "from the beginnings of philosophy, men speculated about infinity. Anaximander (610-547 BC) took it as the basis of his philosophy." (p353) Woods' assertion that Anaximander, who is said to be the first western philosopher to set down philosophical ideas in writing, took infinity "as the basis of his philosophy" gives a misleading impression of Anaximander's views.

Far from suggesting that our universe was infinite, Anaximander said that our universe had come into being in a ball of fire and would pass away. What was revolutionary about the philosophy of Anaximander, particularly from the point of view of dialectical materialism, was precisely his challenge to those who, like Woods, intone: "Thus it has been. Thus it ever will be." Anaximander describes how a "sphere of fire" grew from a "germ, pregnant with hot and cold, [which] separated off from the boundless", forming several rings, from which arose the sun, moon and stars.

For Anaximander, the "heavens and the worlds within them" have a beginning. He also believed they have an end. Anaximander's views, of course, remind us of the Big Bang picture of the birth of the universe, beginning in a hot dense state, a kind of "sphere of fire".

Nevertheless, Anaximander postulated some sort of substratum from which the universe arose in its sphere of fire. "All the heavens and the worlds within them" have arisen from "some boundless nature", Anaximander said. He seemed to use the term, 'the boundless', to describe this substratum. It appears that 'the boundless' represented some kind of inexhaustible source of the creation of matter. But the boundless does not by any means necessarily stand for an infinity of space and time – that interpretation might be no more than an anachronistic extrapolation based on a Newtonian outlook. Some modern translations use the phrase "boundless chaos".

Even so, it is speculated that Anaximander's concept of the boundless arose as an extension of the idea of the immortal Homeric gods. A typical viewpoint states: "Anaximander added two distinctive features to the concept of divinity: his Boundless is an impersonal something and it is not only immortal but also unborn." (*The Internet Encyclopaedia of Philosophy*)

So the origin of the boundless is likely to be associated with concepts of the divine. Thales is thought to have said: "What is the divine? That which has no origin and no end."

Two centuries later Aristotle pointed out, in *Physics* (book one, part seven), that the ancient dialectics of *coming into being* always assumes what he called a "substratum", and we have adopted his term in this review. So from what substratum might our universe have been brought about as if 'from nothing'?

Dialectics and quantum fluctuations in the vacuum of space

Woods discusses such a candidate substratum (indeed, one of the leading candidates) when he discusses the strange subatomic *quantum fluctuations* observed in the apparent vacuum of empty space, in which subatomic particles appear to come into existence fleetingly in opposing pairs, only to recombine and annihilate each other.

What is curious in this connection is that the philosophers of the school which Anaximander and others brought into being, the most ancient, Ionian school, were best known for their concept of *coming into being* and *passing away*. Today's cosmology, in various ways, links a subatomic coming into being and passing away to the sudden coming into being of the universe in the Big Bang.

Towards the beginning of *Reason in Revolt*, Woods mentions in passing what he calls a "restless flux of swirling quantum waves" (p107), when attempting to discuss quantum mechanics. Towards the end of *Reason in Revolt* he correctly quotes from a passage in a now otherwise largely obsolete 1959 book by Banesh Hoffmann: "What we would think of as empty space is a teeming, fluctuating nothingness, with photons appearing from nowhere and vanishing almost as soon as they were born." (Quoted in *Reason in Revolt*, p386)

Woods here correctly points to the curiously dialectical concept of the quantum fluctuations in the vacuum, and compares this with the dialectics of coming into being and passing away, as discussed by Engels in *Anti-Dühring*: "but everything moves, changes, comes into being and passes away." (*Anti-Dühring*, p30)

The theory of quantum fluctuations has been a standard part of quantum mechanics (quantum field theory) for more than fifty years. Yet midway through *Reason in Revolt*, at the pinnacle of its mockery of modern science and the Big Bang, Woods devotes an entire section, *Thoughts in a Vacuum*, to ridiculing this very same idea. (p219) Woods' contradictory positions suggest that he has not understood what he has written.

The interpenetration of opposites

Woods repeats in the abstract: "Everything that exists deserves to perish" but expresses his cosmology like this: "Time, space and motion are the mode of existence of matter, which can neither be created nor destroyed. The universe has existed for all time." (p199) This is not the dialectical viewpoint of the ancient Greek philosophers from whom Hegel developed his dialectics. Woods is here defending Newtonian cosmology. Anaximander conceived that the universe had a beginning and an end but, as a materialist, he always assumed it emerged from some underlying substratum. Ancient philosophers of the school of Thales and Anaximander were materialists and had a dialectical outlook. Anaximander said:

> "Whence things have their origin,
> Thence also their destruction happens."

This means, according to Aristotle: "whatever comes into existence should have an end". This is the origin of the quote from Johann Goethe's Faust, which Engels uses and Woods fondly repeats a few times in *Reason in Revolt*: "Everything that exists deserves to perish" (p141), more correctly expressed as Engels renders it: "All that comes into being deserves to perish."

Anaximander's philosophy of coming into being and passing away reflected turbulent political times in the ancient city state of Miletus. Furthermore, these 'opposites' of coming into being and passing away, of birth and death, creation and destruction, were understood to interpenetrate everything, even our universe itself.

In other words, this ancient school of philosophers believed that the opposites of coming into being and passing away were two integral aspects of everything capable of change: for instance, a person is born and dies, and this mortality is a part of their being. This was the origin of the *unity and interpenetration of opposites*, which Engels summarised so clearly – and which Lenin, following Hegel, considered the central element of dialectics. These opposites, which dialectics says is found in everything which changes, attempt to negate the other, until one finally triumphs and there is a qualitative change – Louis XVI is guillotined, water boils, atoms decay, the living die. There is a passing away and, perhaps, another coming into being. This was called the dialectic of *becoming*.

Aristotle on the heavens

"**A**ristotle would never have made the mistake of talking about a time before time existed," claims Woods. (p209)

Aristotle (384-322BCE),

Woods quotes Aristotle on many occasions throughout *Reason in Revolt*. It is true that Aristotle believed that the universe was eternal. Yet it is not clear how familiar Woods is with Aristotle's writing on time, space or infinity. In general, Aristotle takes a contrary position to that of Woods.

If one takes into account the limitations of his epoch, Aristotle achieved some quite remarkable insights into the nature of our universe. Even though Aristotle developed a logic that effectively usurped the ancient dialectics of Anaximander, Aristotle made occasional use of this ancient dialectics when discussing 'the heavens'.

Woods presents Aristotle's idea of time using this quote from his *Metaphysics*: "Movement can neither come into being nor cease to be: nor can time come into being, or cease to be." Woods sneers: "How much wiser were the great thinkers of the Ancient World than those who now write about 'the beginning of time', and without even smiling!" (p145)

Woods is skating on thin ice. In chapter three of *Physics*, Aristotle discusses the infinite. Aristotle argues, as we have already noted, that there are two sorts of infinity, potential infinity and actual infinity. He concludes very firmly that actual infinity does not exist. It is true, Aristotle explains, that one can always imagine an infinite process, such as in addition. It is not hard to imagine infinity in this sense. This is Aristotle's potential infinity, but it will always remain finite. Something extra can always be added. So:

"there is potentially an infinite... For it will always be possible to take something as extra. Yet the sum of the parts taken will not exceed every determinate magnitude..."

Physics, chapter 3, part 6

Aristotle's conclusion is spelt out very clearly: "... the infinite has a potential existence. But... There will not be an actual infinite." Curiously, Woods does say that Aristotle, "Polemicised against geometers who held that a line segment is composed of infinitely many fixed infinitesimals, or indivisibles." (p354) This means, in simple language, that Aristotle opposed the idea that something can be infinitely divided, or is comprised of an infinite number of parts. Woods does not state this clearly, but rather in general allows the reader to draw the conclusion that Aristotle supports the same views as Woods.

Aristotle was the first western philosopher to clearly explain the materialist position that there is no such thing as the actual infinite, as a separately existing thing. Woods argues that the infinite does exist, and he makes it a central tenet to the philosophy of dialectical materialism. This introduces an element of idealism (in the philosophical rather than the common or popular sense of the term) into *Reason in Revolt* and its interpretation of dialectical materialism, because the infinite is a human idea without any proof of its material existence. It is "beyond all human experience", and yet Woods argues that science should accept this idea as the basis of cosmology.

An idealist approach, in philosophical terms, is one which makes ideas primary and the material world secondary. Idealism explains developments primarily though ideas, and relegates experience to a secondary role, whereas Marxism makes the experience of the material world primary, from which ultimately arises, in a general sense, our ideas about the world. It is important that Woods' interpretation of dialectical materialism on this question is corrected. The philosophical meaning of the terms 'idealism' and 'materialism' is discussed in greater detail in Engels' *Ludwig Feuerbach and the Outcome of Classical German Philosophy*.

Woods takes the position that: "The reason why infinity can be used, and must be used, in modern mathematics is because it corresponds to the existence of infinity in nature itself." (p358) Infinity is not used in this way in mathematics – as Woods concedes later on the same page – because infinity does not correspond to nature itself. Indeed, Aristotle explains that the type of infinities used in mathematics corresponds to his potential infinity. After explaining the illusion of the actual infinity, Aristotle goes on to say:

> "Our account does not rob the mathematicians of their science, by disproving the actual existence of the infinite in the direction of increase... In point of fact they do not need the infinite and do not use it. They postulate only that the finite... may be produced as far as they wish... Hence, for the purposes of proof, it will make no difference to them to have such an infinite instead, while its existence will be in the sphere of real magnitudes."
>
> *Physics*, chapter 3, part 6

By real magnitudes, of course, Aristotle means concrete, measurable quantities that exist in the real world. This issue will be touched on very briefly in the short chapter, *The infinite in mathematics*. But more than mathematicians, scientists tend only to use Aristotle's potential infinity, even among those who defended the idea of an infinite universe. When the Big Bang theory began to gain some adherents, the physicist Fred Hoyle attempted to develop an alternative theory which could explain current cosmological observations on the basis of an infinite universe. In a book popularising his ideas, written in 1955, he simply says: "the word 'infinite' should cause no conceptual difficulties. It simply means that however much of the [universe] we consider there is always more of it." (Fred Hoyle, *Frontiers of Astronomy*, p277) The reader will perhaps recognise that Hoyle's definition of an infinite universe avoids Woods' 'actual' infinity and approximates to Aristotle's potential infinity: it can be "produced as far as [you] wish". Hoyle's alternative theory, the Steady State theory, was not successful.

The infinite and the divine

Aristotle makes an exception of time and of the 'divine' in *On the Heavens*. The divine is taken to be infinite by definition. Aristotle explains that all philosophers agree that anything that changes has an origin in time and is finite, because change is a result of the dialectic of the interpenetration of opposites, of coming into being and passing away. If the heavens (by heavens Aristotle means the cosmos) are capable of change then, according to the dialectic of both Anaximander and Aristotle, they must have had a beginning, and will have an ending, and are finite.

But we do not see the heavens change, says Aristotle (apart from their fixed rotation). He says that the stars are "fixed" in the heavens, and that therefore the heavens must be incorruptible, imperishable, unchanging except for their rotational motion through the heavens, since "a thing whose present state had no beginning and which could not have been other than it was at any previous moment throughout its entire duration, cannot possibly be changed." Whereas, "clearly whatever is generated or destructible is not eternal." (*On the Heavens*, book 1, part 10)

In other words, for Aristotle, dialectics teaches that if there is change in the heavens, the heavens must have an origin and an end. We now know, since Galileo, that there is change in the heavens – that is to say, in the universe. Galileo, incidentally, was convinced that with the evidence before him, Aristotle would have changed his views.

For Aristotle, the heavens' eternity reflected the divine. The reason why Aristotle's aether (the fifth element, the heavens) is eternal, "unaging and unalterable and unmodified", should be clear to "all who believe in the existence of gods at all". Aristotle maintains that the aether is the "seat of all that is divine". (*On the Heavens*, book 1, parts 3 and 9) While the earth was corruptible, the heavens were not. (In the Renaissance and until the beginning of the twentieth century, the term aether, or luminiferous aether, was used to describe the medium through which scientists thought light propagated - an altogether different use of the term.)

Absolute and relative space and time

Woods might have been advised to hesitate before recruiting Aristotle to his cause. He also fails to mention that Aristotle thought the universe, although infinite in time, was a sphere of finite size. Aristotle discusses how concepts of time and space can be meaningful outside this rotating sphere of the heavens. This is fascinating because of its relevance to the concept of the universe that arose from Einstein's relativity, and therefore from modern speculation about into what substratum the matter, time and space of the Big Bang universe might be expanding.

Firstly, we remember that Aristotle argued that within the heavenly spheres, material things fall down to the earth, because the earth happened to be "down", at the centre of the universe. (Aristotle appears even to suggest that the earth is simply an aggregate of everything that has fallen "down".) Fire, on the other hand, heads "up" to the heavens.

This meant that it could be said that for Aristotle time and space were absolute within the bounds of the universe. The earth was the absolute, stationary frame of reference for all motion. For instance, stones fell because the natural place of heavy bodies was the centre of the universe, and that was why the earth was there.

Later, Galileo attacked Aristotle's views. He pointed out that there was not just one universal frame of reference for motion. For instance, if one was to imagine a game of table tennis below decks on an ocean liner, where the ship is travelling in steady, constant motion in calm seas, without rolling from side to side, one can readily predict that the players will not see any difference in the behaviour of the ball compared to a game on *terra firma* – all the laws of motion apply, relative to the frame of reference of the steadily moving boat, just as they do on the shore, relative to which the boat is moving.

This is obvious to us. Today, it is second nature to us that motion is relative, not absolute, even if we are not aware of the laws of physics. Yet to

Aristotle's way of thinking, if the boat was in motion (or, more significantly, if the earth was moving through space), the table tennis balls should behave differently, reflecting the forward motion of the ship (or earth), perhaps as though there was an invisible medium through which they and the boat passed, which affected their motion, sweeping the table tennis balls backwards off the table. This is a concept of absolute space and time.

As we shall show, however, although motion is relative, this does not mean that the motion of the table tennis balls is not an objective, measurable phenomenon – there is no lapse into subjective idealism, which is what Woods associates with the concept of relative space and time.

Before time, outside of space

But outside the 'heavens', the sphere of stars surrounding the Aristotelian universe, Aristotle concludes that there can be no space or time. Nothing exists outside the heavens, Aristotle says, therefore there can be no movement. But since "time is the number of movement" – time is the measure of change – there is no time outside the heavens:

> *"But in the absence of natural body there is no movement, and outside the heaven, as we have shown, body neither exists nor can come to exist. It is clear then that there is neither place, nor void, nor time, outside the heavens."*
>
> On the Heavens, book 1, part 9)

Woods asks the defenders of the Big Bang theory: "So what was there before time? A time when there was no time! The self-contradictory nature of this idea is glaringly obvious." (p210) At least since Aristotle, the answer to the question has not been quite so "obvious". Since Einstein, the question has to be rephrased: What was there 'before' the space-time of our universe?

Woods, however, wishes to distinguish between the measurement of time, which must be relative to some process of change, and the "nature of time itself" (p161), and says: "… in cosmology, the confusion of measurement with the nature of the thing itself leads to disaster in practice." (p158)

But what is this "time itself" or "thing itself" which is to be abstracted from the measurement of change? It is the old Newtonian concept of time. Newton says, in the *Principia*: "Time exists in and of itself and flows equably without reference to anything external." It is truly as if there is somewhere a giant watch, held by a great timekeeper in the sky, keeping track of all celestial matter. We are jumping ahead a little, but for Newton,

Table 1: Schematic summary of Aristotle's views

	Motion		Universe	
	Space	**Time** *	**Space**	**Time**
Aristotle	Absolute	Absolute	Finite	Infinite
	Denied the existence of space and time outside the sphere of the universe			

this timekeeper was god. Einstein did away with the timekeeper. Einstein's universe, it is often said is a "democratic universe" with no dictatorial authority laying down on each and every planet the strict time of the universe. Historically, in any case, the notion of a single time from which all clocks must be set arose in that same historical period which gave rise to Greenwich Mean Time, and should be placed in the context of the politics of Britain's seafaring exploration and conquest of that period.

Woods does not elucidate exactly what "disaster in practice" has occurred as a result of science treating time, since Aristotle, as the measurement of change. Woods concedes, however, that according to this conception: "defining what time is presents a difficulty", which he does not resolve. Time is indeed a complex phenomenon. But this "time itself" which Woods defends is Newtonian absolute time. On the facing page, Woods correctly asserts the opposing view. "It is impossible to regard [space and time] as 'things in themselves'." (p159)

Aristotle's argument that space and time do not exist if there is no matter is, very roughly speaking, an acceptable hypothesis to science today. There is no meaning, in general, to time and space unless there is matter and energy. This is a materialist position, although it can be hard to grasp. But we will leave it to Galileo to demonstrate aspects of this important concept, which he did when he argued – against the followers of Aristotle – that the earth was in motion.

Galileo and the relativity of space

Some elementary scientific errors appear in *Reason in Revolt*, which quite undermine the authority of the author. One is an inability to grasp Galileo's 'principle of relativity', confusing it with Einstein's relativity. Another is to proceed from this failure to the conclusion that modern physics is saturated with "subjective idealism" since, Woods argues, Einstein was always concerned with "the observer" rather than the physical processes taking place independently of any observer in absolute space and time.

Woods misunderstands the term "the observer", as if Einstein means the particular, subjective viewpoint of an individual, rather than a location from which an objective measurement can be taken.

Copernicus' revolution

Galileo Galilei (1564-1642)

Aristotle's heavens appeared incorruptible to western astronomers until the seventeenth century when, in 1609, Galileo constructed his telescope. Galileo discovered that there was change in the spheres, because moons orbited Jupiter, and the moon was pitted with craters and not perfect. This gave rise to a new consciousness among the most advanced thinkers in the Renaissance.

Stars seemed to some to stretch to infinity. But Galileo did not see infinity through his telescope, nor has it ever been seen – only inferred by extrapolation, by the quantitative extension of finite observations.

Galileo defended the Copernican system, which redrew the map of the universe by rearranging the 'perfect spheres' so that the sun rather than the earth was at the centre of the soar system.

Nicolaus Copernicus' famous *On the Revolution of the Heavenly Spheres*, published in 1543, is thought to have invested the word 'revolution' with its 'revolutionary' connotations, in the sense of a complete change or an overthrowing of the old conditions.

In his opening remarks, Copernicus briefly contrasted his revolutionary alternative of an immobile universe in which the earth rotates with the old Aristotelian idea of immense but finite heavens which rotate daily round an immobile earth.

Ptolemy of Alexandria (87-150 CE), Copernicus tells us, had asserted that if the earth rotated, "this movement, which would traverse the total circuit of the earth in twenty-four hours, would necessarily be very headlong and of an unsurpassable velocity." This rotational velocity, Ptolemy says, would have violently torn apart the earth long ago and all the pieces would have "passed beyond the heavens, as is certainly ridiculous". (*On the Revolution of the Heavenly Spheres*, book one, Introduction, point eight, pp22-3)

Copernicus replies that the entire world is supposed to revolve once a day around the earth: "Why didn't [Ptolemy] feel anxiety about the world instead, whose movement must necessarily be of greater velocity?" Would not the much greater rotational movement of the heavenly spheres have torn them apart and thrown them outwards?

Copernicus then asks a quite remarkable question: Have "the heavens become so immense, because an unspeakably vehement motion has pulled them away from the centre, and because the heavens would fall if they came to rest anywhere else?"

This remarkable insight bears comparison with two aspects of the Big Bang theory. Copernicus asks whether the universe is so large because it has expanded from the centre and whether this expansion has prevented the collapse of the heavens, which if they came to rest would be bound to fall back to the centre.

These tentative suggestions remarkably anticipate modern theory. Copernicus seems to present in one brief remark essentially an explanation to the problem of why gravity has not caused the universe to collapse in on itself, a problem which Woods had not fully grasped 450 years later, and an explanation so radical that it was not until the observations of Hubble in 1929-31, which showed that the rapid expansion of the universe would indeed counteract the pull of gravity, that it subsequently struck the scientific world.

Copernicus answers: "[I]f this reasoning were tenable, the magnitude of the heavens would extend infinitely." Perhaps Copernicus has in mind Aristotle's potential infinity – that the heavens would go on expanding indefinitely. But if Copernicus means "infinitely" in the sense Woods presents it (Aristotle's actual infinity), this could only be true if the universe had existed for an infinite period of time. Yet if the universe is expanding "from the centre", it must have began at some finite point in the past.

Galileo's defence of Copernicus

What were Galileo's views on an infinite universe? Just nine years before Galileo began looking through his telescope, in 1600, Giordano Bruno was burned at the stake by the Inquisition, after being tortured for nine years for preaching that the universe was infinite. He refused to recant. So, perhaps not surprisingly, Galileo did not express, or at least did not publish, any views on whether the universe was infinite or not. But he did discover additional contradictions which the idea of infinity leads to, (anticipating some of the concepts of the late nineteenth century mathematician George Cantor, who we discuss very briefly below) and elsewhere notes that infinities "transcend our finite understanding... In spite of this, men cannot refrain from discussing them... we attempt, with our finite minds, to discuss the infinite, assigning to it properties which we give to the finite and limited; but I think this is wrong..." (Galileo, *Dialogues Concerning Two Sciences*, First day, p418)

The 'corruptible heavens' which Galileo viewed through his telescope implied – by Aristotle's own admission – a beginning and end to the universe, and this was bound to disturb all accepted dogmas. In order to defend the theory of Copernicus that the sun, not the earth, was the centre of the solar system, Galileo demonstrated that motion was relative, not absolute, as Aristotle had taught. In the section, *Problem Not Resolved*, Woods says:

> "*Einstein was determined to re-write the laws of physics in such a way that the predictions would always be correct, irrespective of the motions of different bodies, or the 'points of view' which derive from them. From the standpoint of relativity, steady motion on a straight line is indistinguishable from being at rest.*" (p161)

The law that steady motion in a straight line "is indistinguishable from being at rest" is an essential feature of Newton's first law of motion. This was no "re-write" of the laws of physics. Here are Newton's words, published in 1687:

> "*Every body perseveres in its state of rest, or of uniform motion in a right line, unless it is compelled to change that state by forces impressed thereon.*"
>
> *Principia*, Axioms or Laws of Motion

We shall show that, from the point of view of Newton's laws of motion, *rest* and *uniform motion* are equivalent. Woods mistakes what became known as Galileo's *principle of relativity*, enshrined in Newton's first law of motion, for a supposed 're-write' of the laws of physics by Einstein in his theory of relativity, which in fact takes Galileo's principle of relativity as its starting point. Woods even uses the same terms, "rest" "motion" and "line" and yet does not recognise this elementary physics.

Furthermore, Woods seeks to undermine this law of motion, Galileo's principle of relativity, all the time believing it to be a facet of Einstein's relativity, asserting instead the existence of absolute space and time. This leads him to take essentially the same position as the supporters of Aristotle in their dispute with Galileo in his defence of Copernicus. Copernicus, we should add in passing, briefly anticipates Galileo's arguments. (*On the Revolution of the Heavenly Spheres*, book one, Introduction, point five, p23)

What is this fundamental law of physics, the principle of relativity, on which Newton based his first law of motion, and from which Einstein took the name 'relativity'? Let us take a glimpse at what Galileo and Einstein said.

Galileo's thought experiment

The followers of Aristotle's orthodoxy in the early seventeenth century thought that if the earth was travelling round the sun, or rotating, this would cause many very visible effects:

> *"How would birds find their nest again after they had flown from them? Why does a stone thrown up come straight down if the earth underneath it is rotating rapidly to the east?"*
>
> The Galileo Project,
http://galileo.rice.edu/sci/theories/copernican_system.html)

Aristotle himself provided arguments against the notion that the earth moved, since one school of ancient Greek philosophers, led by Pythagoras, proposed that the earth did move. For instance, Aristotle asks, why do "heavy bodies forcibly thrown quite straight upward return to the point from which they started" if the earth has moved in the meantime? (*On The Heavens*, book II, chapter 14)

In the same passage Aristotle also argued that if the earth moved, one would surely see the stars pass by: "… there would have to be passings and turnings of the fixed stars. Yet no such thing is observed. The same stars always rise and set in the same parts of the earth." This was a very powerful argument, not experimentally refuted until stellar parallax was measured by powerful telescopes in the 1800s. (Stellar parallax is the apparent movement of a star caused by viewing it from different positions, for instance, when the earth has moved a sufficient distance in its orbit round the sun.) Galileo could only suppose (correctly) that the stars were at too great a distance for parallax to be observed with the naked eye.

Galileo suggested experiments to prove the followers of Aristotle wrong. Adopting a popular, accessible style and writing in the native language rather than the scholars' Latin, Galileo begins by asking his audience to imagine they are shut up "with some friend in the main cabin below decks on some large ship". While the ship is stationary, Galileo suggests conducting a number of experiments designed to test motion in space, such as throwing and jumping, and setting a bottle to drip into a jar below. Then, he suggests:

> "... *have the ship proceed with any speed you like, so long as the motion is uniform and not fluctuating this way and that. You will discover not the least change in all the effects named, nor could you tell from any of them whether the ship was moving or standing still.*"
>
> Dialogue Concerning the Two Chief World Systems

The water still drips directly into the jar below – it does not fall behind the jar as the ship moves forward steadily. Many people have been below decks on a ship or car ferry, where you cannot see out, and experienced something similar: you cannot be sure if the ferry is moving or not, so long as it is going at a constant velocity. Galileo's point is that a scientist, conducting experiments, could not determine by any experiment whether the ferry or, of course, the earth, was in constant motion or stationary either. This was termed Galileo's *principle of relativity*.

Table 2: Schematic summary of the views of Galileo added to *Table 1*

	Motion		Universe	
	Space	**Time**	**Space**	**Time**
Aristotle	Absolute	Absolute	Finite	Infinite
	Denied the existence of space and time outside the sphere of the universe			
Galileo	Relative	Relative	Finite (assumed)	Infinite (assumed)

Einstein's railway carriage

Einstein deepened Galileo's insights. He discusses Galileo's principle of relativity, which he calls "the fundamental law of the mechanics of [Galileo] Galilei-Newton" at the very beginning of his short popular primer, *Relativity* (first written in 1916 and still in print). He poses two questions:

> *"I stand at the window of a railway carriage which is travelling uniformly, and drop a stone on the embankment, without throwing it. Then, disregarding the influence of the air resistance, I see the stone descend in a straight line. A pedestrian who observes the misdeed from the footpath notices that the stone falls in a parabolic curve. I now ask: Do the 'positions' traversed by the stone lie 'in reality' on a straight line or on a parabola? Moreover, what is meant here by motion 'in space'?"*
>
> Einstein, *Relativity*, p9

Einstein reminds us that Galileo and Newton (in respect of his first law of motion) have shown that in reality both views are equally valid. Both views, furthermore, are objective descriptions of reality; neither are merely subjective impressions. Despite what Woods maintains, the subjective thoughts or impressions of individuals do not come into it.

Woods argues: "Einstein regretted his earlier subjective idealism, or 'operationalism', which demanded the presence of an observer to determine natural processes." (p167) Einstein never demanded the presence of an observer to determine natural processes. It is a "complete misinterpretation of Einstein's ideas" as Woods himself says slightly earlier (p163), without appearing to understand what he says. Einstein proceeds to re-phrase his own words this way:

> *"The stone traverses a straight line relative to a system of coordinates rigidly attached to the carriage, but relative to a system of coordinates rigidly attached to the ground (embankment) it describes a parabola."*
>
> *Relativity*, p10

What concerns us is the relative positions of the stone, as measured according to two different system of coordinates, or frames of reference, one moving and one stationary – the train and the platform.

But does one frame of reference offer a correct description, while the other is merely secondary? No, they are both correct. At first, we may be tempted to say that the pedestrian has the correct view or, to put the same thing another way, that the stone, as measured according to the frame of reference of the earth, is the correct measurement, because the pedestrian is the 'stationary' one, standing on the 'stationary' earth.

But the earth is not stationary. We must keep in mind that in the few seconds it took for the stone to fall, the earth and the stone have travelled perhaps thirty kilometres or more around the sun. Why take the earth as the correct or absolute reference point? In addition, the sun itself travels round our galaxy, and our galaxy is moving in a complex gravitational dance with our local cluster of galaxies. And all independent clusters of galaxies in the universe are moving away from us at great speed, in proportion to their distance from us.[1]

Whose space is the correct space? From the point of view of physics each view, each measurement, whether from the railway carriage, the footpath, or the Andromeda galaxy, is equally valid. According to the Newtonian laws of motion which begin with Galileo's insight (and which Newton acknowledged), the view from Andromeda is just as valid as the view from the train.

According to classical Newtonian physics, we have no trouble at all translating the measurements of one frame of reference into that of another. They have a very simple, physical relationship. Suppose the train is moving at twenty miles an hour relative to the footpath frame of reference. A passenger is walking towards the front of the train at three miles an hour in the railway carriage, or to put it another way, relative to the railway carriage frame of reference, the passenger is moving at three miles an hour. By simple addition, we say that the passenger is moving at twenty-three miles an hour relative to the footpath frame of reference – the speed of the train plus the speed of the passenger in the carriage.

We make this rather obvious point to make clear that no-one, whether Galileo, Newton or Einstein, is suggesting that, because the measurements are, in the common idiom, relative to the observer, these measurements are "subjective" in some way, or that physics has wallowed in subjective idealism ever since Galileo, which is the unintended essence of Woods' claim.

However, Einstein realised that these calculations fail to take into consideration the speed of light. When we observed the train moving, we did so with the aid of light. But light does not travel instantaneously as our Newtonian calculation above assumed but at a definite speed. Furthermore, light has very unexpected properties. It is only once we have learnt about the strange qualities of light and have taken them into account that we can start to discuss Einstein's universe. (In order to calculate the real transformation of the speed of the passenger relative to the carriage into his or her speed as measured from the platform, an equation associated with the physicist Hendrik Lorenz must be used, which takes the strange properties of light into account: the *Lorenz transformation*.)

What is space?

Asking what is meant by motion in space, Einstein says we "cannot form the slightest conception" of what 'space' means, since it seems to have two quite different values according to the person on the train and the pedestrian. Instead, he reconstructs the description of the stone's trajectory in terms of two systems of coordinates – the moving train and the footpath. He concludes:

> "*there is no such thing as an independently existing trajectory but only a trajectory relative to a particular body of reference.*"
>
> Relativity, p10

Therefore, in popular terminology, the motion of the stone dropped from the train must always be described according to some 'observer' – a particular body of reference – the earth, the train, the sun, etc, to have any meaning.

This is what Woods considers to be subjective idealism. But Engels also understood that there was no such thing as an independently existing trajectory. When Engels first conceived of writing about the dialectics of nature, in 1873, he began by noting the following:

> "*1. The first, simplest form of motion is the mechanical form, pure change of place:*
> *a) Motion of a single body does not exist* – [it can be spoken of] *only in a relative sense...*"
>
> Dialectics of Nature, p329

In words, Woods sometimes denies and sometimes echoes the idea that time and space are bound up with matter. But when he argues that, "Time and space are properties of matter, and cannot be conceived of separately from matter" (p146), it becomes clear from the context that Woods is not embracing Einstein's theory of relativity, but essentially arguing that if a body is travelling at a certain speed, this motion through space and time is an inherent property of that body, without reference to any other body, in other words, not relative to it. In this sense, it is an expression of absolute space and time.

The earth's motion must be judged in relation to other bodies, such as the sun. Taken as a single body, the earth's motion "does not exist", as Engels puts it. We may treat the earth, in accordance with our day-to-day earthbound experience, as stationary. The earth's creatures do not experience its motion because space is relative. Remember that all we are discussing here is Galileo's principle of relativity and Einstein's discussion of it. But Woods rejects this, thinking he is rejecting Einstein's "subjective idealism".

Clocks, twins and time

Despite the fact that he calls Einstein's special relativity "one of the greatest achievements of science" (p160), Woods proceeds, sometimes insidiously and sometimes openly, to attempt to denigrate Einstein's relativity, particularly in the sections *Problem Not Resolved*, and *Idealist Interpretations*. (Einstein's 'special relativity' deals only with the special case of motion unaffected by gravity or acceleration. His 'general relativity' includes gravity.)

Woods discusses the famous 'twins' example, where one twin goes on a high-speed intergalactic journey and returns having aged less than her earthbound twin. Woods' treatment is impeded by his failure to grasp Galileo's principle of relativity. Let us see how Galileo's science contradicts *Reason in Revolt*.

Woods begins:

> "*A controversial idea here is the prediction that a clock in motion will keep time more slowly than one that is stationary. However it is important to understand that this effect becomes noticeable at extraordinarily high speeds, approaching the speed of light.*" (p163)

There is much that is wrong here but, above all, the effect of motion on the timekeeping of clocks is not "controversial", it is incontrovertibly proved (as Woods admits elsewhere). For instance, navigation systems using the Global Positioning System (GPS) constantly make use Einstein's special and general theory of relativity in about a dozen distinct types of calculations, in order to ensure the accuracy of their results, twenty-four hours a day. It is quite misleading for Woods to witheringly assert: "Unlike special relativity, experimental tests which have been carried out on [the general theory of relativity] are not very many." (p172) Fifty years ago Woods' assertions were true. The reader may have noticed already that *Reason in Revolt* is trapped in a kind of fifty-year-old time warp. (This is true for the second half of the book also, which we do not discuss in this review.)

In *Einstein's Universe*, Nigel Calder describes the definitive experiment on this question, carried out in 1971 using four robust atomic clocks, which were placed aboard regularly scheduled commercial passenger jet aircrafts which took them right around the world. "One circumnavigation was made eastwards and one westwards, both journeys taking about three days. The result of the experiment was that the clocks no longer agreed about the time of day." The clocks were compared to similarly highly accurate atomic clocks which remained at the US Naval Observatory in Washington DC. (*Einstein's Universe*, p60)

The two experimenters, JC Hafele and Richard Keating, had predicted a loss of 40 nanoseconds eastbound, and the clocks did indeed lose time, although it was slightly larger, at 59 nanoseconds. Westbound the experimenters predicted a gain of 275 nanoseconds and the clocks gained 273 nanoseconds, a very close agreement indeed.

"In Newton's universe, there would be no accounting for the discrepancies in such highly reliable instruments," Calder remarks. Since then, subsequent experiments have tested the theory to far greater precision.

Woods proceeds to admit that this 'time dilation' effect, as it is called, has indeed been observed, and now objects: "The whole question hinges upon whether the changes, observed in rates of atomic clocks, also apply to the rate of life itself." (p164) Woods' line of argument could only arise if he has not grasped Galileo's principle of relativity, since it does not matter in the least what is moving – living organisms or mechanical clocks – the point is their steady motion is measured relative to a stationary observer (another frame of reference, an earthbound twin, etc). It is only relative to earthbound clocks that the clocks on the spaceship run slow.

In the section *Idealist interpretations*, Woods says, "it is not easy to see" how "the process of aging" of the astronaut twin can be "fundamentally affected either by velocity or gravitation, except that extremes of either can cause material damage to living organisms." He continues:

> "*If it were possible to slow down the rate of metabolism in the way predicted, so that, for example, the heart-beat would slow to one every twenty minutes, the process of aging would presumably be correspondingly slower. It is, in fact, possible to slow down the metabolism, for example, by freezing. Whether this would be the effect of travelling at very high speeds, without killing the organism, is open to doubt.*" (p165)

Relativity, of course, makes no prediction about slowing down a person's metabolism. It is not a biological science. But can extremes of velocity "cause material damage to living organisms" as Woods appears to believe? The followers of Aristotle's orthodoxy in the early seventeenth century thought that if the earth was "travelling at very high speed" it would cause very visible effects, and ridiculed the idea mercilessly. Yet the entire earth's population is going round the sun at roughly thirty kilometres a second, or one ten-thousandth of the speed of light.

Woods feels that the time dilation effect on "life itself" is "open to doubt" because he is convinced that travelling at very high speeds is injurious to life. Would not this very high speed "kill the organism" or at least cause some "material damage to living organisms" just as Woods ponders it might? Does our metabolism slow down? It does not, no matter how fast we travel at a steady velocity, because space is relative, as Galileo explained.

We must emphasis here another point that Woods fails to grasp. What is being discussed here is constant velocity or steady motion in a straight line. Woods also uses this term: "From the standpoint of relativity, steady motion on a straight line is indistinguishable from being at rest." (p161) Einstein's special theory of relativity, written in 1905, takes the special case of steady motion in a straight line (velocity), and excludes acceleration. Acceleration is quite different to steady motion. An accelerating jet fighter plane can generate enough g-forces to swiftly kill the pilot. Einstein's later general theory of relativity, published in 1916, deals with acceleration, and he showed that acceleration too can affect time and space.

The entire point in the twins example is that the clocks and heart-beat of the space traveller moving at high speed are slow only relative to her twin on the earth. The motion of the spaceship is not an absolute motion, a spaceship which has the "property" of moving at high speed. Although it must have accelerated to its current speed, now it is cruising in steady motion it is only moving at its current high speed relative to the earth from which it departed. Relative to her frame of reference, the astronaut is stationary, and her life processes are unaffected by her relative motion as she floats weightlessly inside her craft. She could "survive thousands of years into the future" (p164) but only as measured from the earth, only into the future of the earth, not as measured from the spaceship, where she will live a normal life span – disappointing as that may be. It is clear that Woods cannot consistently grasp Galileo's principle of relativity here, let alone the 'twins' example itself in relation to Einstein's relativity (which is more involved than can be adequately discussed here).

The discussion of Einstein's relativity in *Reason in Revolt* never grasps the seventeenth century scientific debate between Galileo and Aristotle's supporters, and at no point clearly recognises the validity of Galileo's arguments (as Engels certainly did) or of Newton's first law of motion. Essentially, in this respect, *Reason in Revolt* sides with those who supported Aristotle's views of a stationary earth, at the centre of the celestial spheres.

Woods makes a further error when, as discussed above, he asked whether "the changes, observed in rates of atomic clocks, also apply to the rate of life itself". Woods tries to draw a distinction between processes taking place in humans or other living things and those in inanimate objects moving at high speeds. This is an unintentional departure from materialism, since it suggests humans or living things have a special, non-physical (and by implication therefore spiritual) essence which does not necessarily always obey the laws of physics by which material things are bound.

Criticising modern cosmological applications of Einstein's relativity, Woods intones, "Here the study of philosophy becomes indispensable" (p216) but he has not grasped the problem, the most basic, elementary physics and, in fact, cannot escape from Aristotelian or Newtonian concepts of absolute space and time, on which his philosophical criticism of modern science is based. Philosophy is no use when you have no grasp of your subject.

Einstein applied the same relativity principle to time, but these considerations still do not yet depart, in essence, from classical Newtonian laws of motion. The issues that Einstein addressed which brought about an entirely new understanding of the universe will be briefly touched on later.[2]

1   For those familiar with these concepts: according to the satellite COBE's 1996 measurements, our solar system is moving at roughly one thousandth the speed of light (about 300 kilometres per second) in the direction of the constellation Leo, relative to the cosmic background radiation. http://arxiv.org/PS_cache/astro-ph/pdf/9601/9601151.pdf. Our local cluster of galaxies is travelling at twice this speed in the direction of the constellation Crater. http://www.arxiv.org/abs/astro-ph/0210165 (NB: Incidentally, unlike velocity, rotational movement can be determined by experiment.)

2   But we are justified in considering so closely Galileo's contribution since, as the physicist Hermann Bondi once said, "I always say that Einstein's contribution has a name for being difficult, but it is quite wrong. Einstein's contribution is very easy to understand, but unfortunately it rests on the theories of Galileo and Newton which are very difficult to understand!" (Quoted by Gleik, *Issac Newton*, p 200)

Newton: belief and contradiction

opernicus' theory led to fresh speculation about the nature of the universe. The modern concept of an infinite universe first began to emerge here, linked to religious expressions of an infinite god.

Newton did not prove but merely asserted that the world was infinite. The idea of an infinite universe was undoubtedly extrapolated at least in part from the belief that to the vast quantities of stars and space that Galileo saw through his telescope there must be added vast quantities more, without end, to the glory of god.

The universe, Woods writes,

"was rapidly 'expanded' – in the minds of men – and... is now thought to measure tens of billions of light years across, and time will show that even the present calculations are nowhere near big enough. For the universe, as Nicolas of Cusa and others thought, is infinite." (p184)

Sir Isaac Newton (1643-1727)

Recent calculations suggest that the universe is at least 156 billion light-years wide. The German cardinal, Nicolas of Cusa (1401-1464), anticipated Copernicus (1473-1543) by nearly a century, proposing that the earth rotated and, as Woods rightly points out, argued that the universe was infinite.

In 2002, Woods appeared to have changed his estimation of the width of the universe. In his preface to the 2002 USA edition of *Reason in Revolt*, Woods offers his support to a mainstream re-working of the old speculative cyclical Big Bang theory. The idea that the universe goes through cycles consisting of a Big Bang followed billions of years later by a Big Crunch had been first suggested in the 1930s, soon after observation suggested our universe had a hot dense origin a few billion years ago. Woods supports reports carried in the popular media of prominent physicists Paul Steinhardt and Neil Turok's 2002 version of this theory, saying that it was fully compliant with dialectical materialism, subject to experimental proof, because these two physicists, at least in their popular presentation, talked about a universe infinite in time.

Steinhardt and Turok's cyclical big bang theory proposes that the universe goes through a perpetual motion of Big Bangs followed by what they term "big splats" as the universe reaches the end of the cycle. Woods, in 2002, thus continues to defend an infinity of time, but not an infinity of space, which expands and contracts perpetually with each cycle, according to the model. Are we to conclude that Woods now concedes that dialectical materialism does not prescribe to the universe an infinity of space, as he originally asserted in 1995 when *Reason in Revolt* was published?

Nicolas of Cusa argued that the universe is infinite because god is infinite. Today the concept of an infinite god in infinite space is a commonplace concept. Nicolas of Cusa developed this concept from the ideas originating with the ancient Greek idealist philosopher Plato and the school of philosophy which Plato established. Cusa argued against the existing scholasticism based on the Aristotelian model of the finite universe, which the Catholic church embraced at that time.

Thomas Diggs (1546-95), an early supporter of Copernicus, was the first modern European astronomer to argue that the universe was infinite. He said it reflected the greatness of god, although the church at the time objected that an infinite universe left no room for heaven. This theme, that god was infinite and that the universe should reflect this, began to be adopted by the most far-sighted 'theorists' of the day, who had broken from Aristotle's influence, although it was not until the end of the nineteenth century that it became an uncontested commonplace viewpoint.

William Shakespeare, a family friend of Diggs, reflected the conflicting views of the universe in many allusions (some quite obscure) in *Hamlet*. John Barrow cites, in *The Infinite Book*, a mention of the concept of infinite space in one of Hamlet's declamations: "I could be bounded in a nutshell, and count myself a king of infinite space." (*Hamlet*, Act II, scene ii)

Speculation about an infinite universe lacked a basis in fact, but was linked to abstract religious considerations. The old concept that the universe consisted of concentric spheres began to break down. Giordano Bruno (1548-1600) was burned at the stake after refusing to recant his belief in an infinite universe. He claimed that there was no limit to the power of god and that god could have created an infinite universe.

"Thus is the excellence of God magnified and the greatness of his kingdom made manifest; he is glorified not in one, but in countless suns; not in a single earth, a single world, but in a thousand thousand, I say in an infinity of worlds."

On the Infinite Universe and Worlds, 1584

Bruno introduced many ideas that became commonplace in the later centuries, such as that space with its infinite worlds extends without limit in all directions and it has no central point. Bruno also suggested that life exists on other planets. Bruno was a Neo-Platonist mystic with no understanding of astronomy, and today the concept of an infinite universe is often credited to Copernicus. What is called the Copernican principle – that the sun-centred solar system occupies no special place in the universe, and that the sun is one of many stars – is perhaps better credited to Bruno.

Among Newton's influences was his contemporary, Henry More (1614–87). More was one of the leading philosophers of the influential group of philosophical 'divines', now known as the Cambridge Platonists, who broke with Aristotelian tradition. More believed that space was infinite, since infinite, immaterial space is analogous to god, who was an infinitely extended spirit.

In 1654, just a few years before Newton observed an apple fall and wondered whether the same attraction of the apple to the earth might keep the moon in tow, William Charleton wrote, in opposition to Aristotle, that time "flow[s] on eternally in the same calm and equal tenor" and is distinct from any measure of it. (Stanford University's *Stanford Encyclopaedia of Philosophy* website: Newton's Views on Space, Time and Motion) These views on time, once again, can be attributed to the influence of the thoroughly idealist philosopher Plato.

Newton's infinite, absolute space and time

But it was Newton who most certainly set in motion what became our 'common sense' ideas about the universe, until the advent of Einstein's theories and then the Big Bang cosmology. Newton's general views on infinite time and space were essentially the same as these contemporaries. In the closing discussion in his *Principia*, Newton explains why he regards space and time to be infinite and absolute:

> "*by existing always and every where, [god] constitutes duration and space. Since every particle of space is always, and every indivisible moment of duration is every where, certainly the Maker and Lord of all things cannot be never and no where.*"
>
> *Principia*, book three, *General Scholium*, p1158

For Newton, infinite absolute space was a meaningful concept for these reasons. Gottfried Leibniz, one of the most prominent of Newton's scientific contemporaries in Europe, opposed this view. There was a long-running, bitter dispute between the two. Newton must take most of the blame for the bitterness, but the debate extended over a wide range of issues and continued for decades among the most prominent scientists of Europe.

Woods cannot, in fact, distinguish between Newton and Einstein on these questions. Woods argues that "the greatness of Einstein" was to reveal the relative character of "the 'absolute truths' of classical Newtonian mechanics", but adds that the "relative aspect of time, was, however, not new. It was thoroughly analysed by Hegel". (p147) This view cannot be supported. The examples Woods gives have no bearing on the meaning of Einstein's relativity in relation to time, the origin of which will be touched on very briefly in its proper historical context. Woods later gives examples such as: "A year on earth is not the same as a year on Jupiter" (p158), and so forth, in a series of irrelevant commonplaces, which never escape from Newtonian physics.

Contradictions in Newton's beliefs: absolute space

In fact, Newton grasped these issues more profoundly since he also understood Galileo's principle that we experience space as relative, and admitted that he had failed to provide evidence of his belief in absolute space.

In the opening *Scholium*, or discussion, of his *Principia*, Newton asserts: "Absolute space, in its own nature, without regard to anything external, remains always similar and immovable." He also discusses relative space, which he assumes takes place in absolute unmovable space. "Relative space is some movable dimension or measure of absolute space." But Newton admits that absolute space cannot be detected: "… the parts of that immovable [absolute] space, in which these motions are performed, do by no means come under the observation of our senses." Newton ruminates that "the thing is not altogether desperate" and provides a range of arguments and suggests experiments that might detect absolute space.

But Newton's absolute space is undetectable because the Newtonian concept of absolute space is false. It is relative space on which Newton's laws of motion are based.

Problems with Newton's universal gravity

Newton admitted he had no idea what formed the basis of the mysterious "action at a distance" by which his universal gravity binds tiny planets

Table 3: Schematic summary of Newton's views added to *Table 2*

	Motion		Universe		Infinity
	Space	**Time**	**Space**	**Time**	
Aristotle	Absolute Denied the existence of space and time outside the sphere of the universe	Absolute	Finite	Infinite	Denied actual infinite
Galileo	Relative	Relative	Finite (assumed)	Infinite (assumed)	Showed paradoxes of infinite
Newton	Absolute Laws of motion based on relative space & time; assumed absolute space & time real but undetected	Absolute	Infinite	Infinite	God as Infinite

in the vastness of space in their orbit round the sun. In his concluding *General Scholium* of his *Principia*, he merely says: "But hitherto I have not been able to discover the causes of those properties of gravity from the phenomena, and I frame no hypotheses." More frankly, in a letter to Richard Bentley in 1693, Newton writes that action at a distance is "so great an absurdity that I believe no man who has in philosophical matters a competent faculty of thinking can ever fall into it". (Quoted in *Newton: Philosophical Writings*, Cambridge University Press, p102) Woods falls into it.

Newton's rival, Leibniz, famously said that Newton's universal gravity had an "occult quality". "The fundamental principle of reasoning", Leibniz emphasised, "is, nothing is without cause," yet Newton, "is admitting that no cause underlies the truth that a stone falls towards the Earth." (Quoted by James Gleick, *Issac Newton*, p156) Newton did not necessarily disagree. It is now widely recognised that Newton spent a great deal of time on what would now be classed as the occult, particularly alchemy. The economist John Maynard Keynes, who acquired many of Newton's writings on alchemy, stated: "Newton was not the first of the age of reason: he was the last of the magicians." (*The Collected Writings of John Maynard Keynes*, Volume X, pp 363-4)

The reason he frames no hypotheses, Newton says, in the above quoted passage from his *Principia*, is because hypotheses, "whether metaphysical or physical, whether of occult qualities or mechanical, have no place in experimental philosophy". Science had not yet fully separated itself from alchemy, astrology and the occult. Newton rules out neither mechanical nor occult qualities to explain the action of gravity at a distance but he does rule out hypotheses. He was searching for proof, not hypotheses, and he was not able to discover any explanation for his universal gravitation, despite a considerable amount of investigation into the occult. Nevertheless, Keynes is not entirely correct. The *Principia*, more than any other work of the era, was defining the new ground of experimental physics and mathematical proof and, in addition, replacing an interventionist god with a god that designed the physical universe along rational and universal principles only at the moment of creation.

The mechanists of the period were "labouring to banish occult influences – mysterious action without contact," James Gleick points out in his biography of Newton. Yet "Action at a distance, across the void, smacked of magic. Occult explanations were supposed to be forbidden." (*Issac Newton*, p96, p142) How did gravity mysteriously act on bodies completely remote from them, with no intervening substance? Hegel chides Newton for not developing laws which go beyond a mere description of the actual mechanics of gravity's effects. "Even Newton's proofs," he says, somewhat stretching the point, are "nothing more than mere jugglery and window-dressing" (*Science of Logic*, p273), especially those which merely gave mathematical expression to the motion of the planets which Johannes Kepler had already discovered.

It was Einstein's general theory of relativity that eventually resolved this paradox, by showing how space and time are bent ("warped") by mass and energy. It is this warped path in space-time that the planets follow. There is no force acting at a distance through the void on the planets. The planets do not depart from Newton's first law, which says that no object will depart from a straight path unless a force compels it to change direction. No force is acting on the planets to make them move from a straight path, but the space-time they inhabit is itself bent, as viewed from the perspective of the solar system, and all paths bend with it. In the dark vastness of space, the planets follow curved paths because space and time are bent by the sun's gravitational effect. It is a stunning discovery, both mathematically and experimentally proven.

No longer could space and time, mass and energy, be treated as absolutely independent of one another. The sun's great mass dimples the space-time around it so that the planets ploughing through space-time naturally follow the curvature of space-time around the sun. Thus Newton's occult force which acts at a distance is replaced with a material effect. In scientific terminology, the Newtonian term 'gravitational force' is replaced with the term 'gravitational effect'. Yet Woods disparages Einstein's general theory of relativity and wants to return to Newton. To save science from mysticism, he wants to deliver it to the occult.

The near century that lies between Galileo's discovery of the moons of Jupiter and Newton's publication of the *Principia* is a remarkable period. Galileo demolished Aristotle and showed that there was corruption in the spheres – the universe must have had a beginning and an end. He further showed that space was relative and that the earth went round the sun, and stood on trial before the Inquisition. Eight decades later Newton reasserted that space and time were absolute and re-established a universe that was infinite in space and time, so long as god was the Prime Mover.

Problems of the infinite: starlight

Not all scientists in Newton's time, however, accepted an infinity of space and time. Newton's contemporary, Edmund Halley, who was the first to calculate the orbit of a comet using Newton's laws, attempted to refute "the ancient notion, some have of late entertained, of the eternity of all things". (Quoted in Stephen Jay Gould, *Eight Little Piggies*, p175)

This did not mean, as has been supposed, that Halley was a creationist. On the contrary, Halley's refusal to take The Bible literally caused John Flamsteed, the Astronomer Royal, to oppose his appointment to a post at Oxford University, saying he would "corrupt the youth of the university".

Halley required evidence, and there was neither evidence for the biblical creation, nor for an infinite universe. There was evidence against in both cases, however. Halley noted a serious contradiction in the concept of an infinite universe:

> *"I have heard it urged that if the number of fixed stars were more than finite, the whole superficies of their apparent sphere would be luminous.*
> Quoted by John Barrow, *The Infinite Book*, p151

In other words, if the universe was infinite and therefore populated with an infinity of stars, the night sky should be brilliantly illuminated, as if it were day. This contradiction was rediscovered by Wilhelm Olbers (1758-1840), and became known as Olbers' paradox. Despite many attempts, no explanation of this paradox (such as interstellar dust, distance, etc), in the context of a universe infinite in space and time, has been successful.

Suppose you are in a deep forest with an infinite amount of trees. Every line of sight soon ends up at a tree. But if you are in a small wood with a finite amount of scattered trees, every line of sight does not end up at a tree.

We live in a universe that has a finite amount of scattered stars and galaxies, with great voids where there are no stars or galaxies.

Problems of the infinite: gravitational collapse

Woods contrasts his version of infinite space with that of Einstein's, which he says was "closed" and "static". This is not true. Einstein's theory allows for both an open and a closed universe, and makes no claims that the universe is static. It was Newton who developed a view of an infinite universe in a "static or a permanent state of equilibrium", as Woods puts it.

If space is finite, Newton correctly argues, gravity would make stars move "towards all the matter on the inside and by consequence fall down to the middle of the whole space and there compose one great spherical mass."

But, Newton reasons, in infinite space it might be possible to position each star so precisely that it is equally attracted by all on all sides. Then, argued Newton, the stars would not be able to fall into one another. But only a divine power could position the stars so exactly, as Newton explains:

> "*but that there should be a Central particle so accurately placed in the middle as to be always equally attracted on all sides and thereby continue without motion, seems to me a supposition fully as hard as to make the sharpest needle stand upright on its point upon a looking glass. For if the very mathematical centre of the central particle be not accurately in the very mathematical centre of the attractive power of the whole mass, the particle will not be attracted equally on all sides…*"

> "*Yet I grant it possible, at least by a divine power… they would continue in that posture without motion for ever, unless put into new motion by the same power.*"
>
> Letters to Richard Bentley, 1692-3

No scientific solution (as opposed to a spiritual one which invoked the hand of god to initially set things in motion) could be found to this apparent contradiction between the theory of gravity, Newton's greatest scientific discovery, and an infinite universe, Newton's unshakable belief.

Newton saw that the problem of gravitational collapse is posed for any system, finite or infinite, however dynamic or static, so long as it contains matter. It makes no difference if there is, as Woods at one point supposes, a "continual process of movement and change, which involves periodic explosions, expansion and contraction, life and death". (p189) Or whether,

"Long periods of apparent equilibrium are interrupted by violent explosions." (p215) Whichever scenario you choose, continual movement or interrupted equilibrium, neither scenario avoids the issue. Gravitational attraction between places of equilibrium, or expansion and contraction, would pull them together over a period of time that would be a blink of an eye compared to an infinity of time, as Newton foresaw.

What is the answer to the conundrum of gravitational collapse? Why has all the matter in space not collapsed in on itself in the universe?

Expansion of space

The definitive answer came in 1929-31 with Edwin Hubble's earth-shaking discoveries. Hubble provided the first evidence that the universe is expanding. Using powerful telescopes, Hubble showed that galaxies are generally receding from one another and from us, not simply moving this way and that. Hubble also noticed another remarkable fact that was far more significant.

It appeared that space itself was expanding. Hubble's results showed a universe expanding in such a way that clusters of galaxies move away from ours at a speed that increases with distance. Galaxies are not all receding from us at around 700 miles per second – 2.5 million miles per hour – as Woods nonchalantly says. (p155) In general, at 100 million light-years away, galaxy clusters are moving away from us at 5.5 million miles per hour, while those at 200 million light years are moving away at twice as fast, at 11 million miles an hour, and at 300 million lights years away, they are moving away three times as fast. (Brian Greene, *The Fabric of the Cosmos*, p229)

Why is this? If a "great explosion", as Woods calls the Big Bang (p189), had torn apart some pre-existing primordial mass – the equivalent on a much larger scale of a star going supernova – then the speeds of the different objects observed would tend to be related to their masses, with the lightest pieces being thrown further with the greatest motion, compared to the heaviest. There would at least be a great variation in speeds. Hubble did not find this. Instead, Hubble saw the universal orchestration of an orderly expansion. Hubble recognised that this could only be explained if what was expanding was space itself.

In the same way, when a cake stuffed with raisins rises in the oven, the raisins (the equivalent of galaxies) move apart from one another in a simple relationship determined by the surrounding cake mixture – in particular, the amount of self-raising flour in the mixture. If the cake explodes, one sees quite a different dynamic.

It is this expansion of space which is such a significant indication of a hot, dense origin of the universe and of space-time itself. The evidence is not consistent with what Woods calls a "great explosion" taking place in infinite space and time. (The term 'Big Bang' is a mischievous misnomer, which amuses astrophysicists but trips up Woods. Ironically, it was first coined by Fred Hoyle, who believed to the end of his life that the universe was infinite in space and time but was forced to admit that the Big Bang was the only existing satisfactory explanation for astronomical experimental data. Hoyle used the term derisively, and was perfectly aware of how misleading it was.)

Where gravity is strong enough to counteract it, it is thought that this expansion of space is halted. Within galaxies and some clusters of galaxies, for instance, this expansion of space is overcome and gravity has taken over. Nevertheless, as a whole, the universe is expanding and gravity has been unable to overcome this expansion, and thus has been unable to cause the entire universe to collapse into "one great spherical mass".

By the end of the nineteenth century, so ingrained in common sense was the concept of an infinite universe (whether containing within it regions of expansion and contraction or equilibrium), that even Einstein, who seemed to question every common sense conception, did not at first question it, and tried to solve the problems which Newton pondered. Only hard scientific evidence provided by Hubble and reinforced by countless observations since, caused Einstein to abandon the concept of an infinite universe.

Woods does not seem to understand the nature of the problem: "The Achilles' heel of Einstein's static, closed universe is that it would inevitably collapse in on itself because of the force of gravity." (p204) Woods does not seem to realise that this is also the Achilles' heel of his universe where "Long periods of apparent equilibrium are interrupted by violent explosions."

In his 1917 paper, *Cosmological Considerations on the General Theory of Relativity*, Einstein considers the problem, and ruminates that "if we really have to regard the universe as being of infinite spatial extent", then, "It seems hardly possible to surmount these difficulties on the basis of the Newtonian theory." This is because Newton's infinite universe suffers the same Achilles' heel.

Einstein suggests that, "if it were possible to regard the universe as a continuum which is finite (closed) with respect to spatial dimensions", a solution can be found, but only if there was a repulsive force, which he termed a cosmological constant, which could counteract gravity.

After learning that the universe was expanding so that gravity is current-ly being overcome by the expansion, Einstein called the addition of the cosmological constant to his general theory of relativity his "greatest mistake". A cosmological constant could not in any case keep the universe in equilibrium, it was found.

Why does Woods suggest that the problem of gravitational collapse affects only a closed universe? Is he obscuring from *Reason in Revolt's* readers this significant and widely known contradiction: that a universe infinite in time and space would inevitably collapse under its own weight? Or is he simply unfamiliar with the science?

Kant's cosmology and Engels' commentary

n the eighteenth century, Immanuel Kant speculated on the nature of the universe. His ideas had a remarkable influence and he is still cited today, for instance, as one of the first to suggest that there are galaxies other than our Milky Way, in his book, *Universal Natural History and the Theory of Heavens* published in 1755.

In the later *Critique of Pure Reason*, and in the *Prolegomena*, Kant gives the first of his cosmological 'antinomies', or contradictions, as follows:

"Thesis: The world has a beginning in time and space (a limit).
Antithesis: The world is spatially and temporally infinite.

Prolegomena, Section 51

Kant's cosmological antinomies, which began by counter-posing the concepts of a finite and an infinite universe, were the announcement of the conscious reintroduction of dialectics into philosophy.

Following Kant's reintroduction and re-interpretation of the dialectics which originated in ancient Greece, Hegel immersed himself in a study of ancient Greek philosophy as a student. Later Hegel recognised that there were not just four cosmological antinomies, or contradictions, as Kant supposed, but opposing tendencies in everything. Engels terms this the "interpenetration of opposites".

Kant's theory of the evolution of the solar system from a "nebulous" state, a gaseous cloud, is still credited in science today for revolutionising our understanding of the solar system's formation.

"Kant began his career by resolving the stable Solar system of Newton and its eternal duration, after the famous initial impulse had once been given, into the result of a historical process, the formation of the Sun and all the planets out of a rotating, nebulous mass. From this, he at the same time drew the conclusion that, given this origin of the Solar system, its future death followed of necessity. His theory, half a century later, was established mathematically by Laplace, and half a century

after that, the spectroscope proved the existence in space of such incandescent masses of gas in various stages of condensation.

Engels, *Socialism, Utopian and Scientific*, Selected Works, p408

Is this quoted anywhere in *Reason in Revolt?* If so, we must have missed it. Engels appears to suggest a universe with a history in time – a beginning and an end. Woods mentions Kant's theory twice, but fails to draw from it the conclusions that Engels does. Engels calls Kant's insight "the greatest advance made by astronomy since Copernicus. For the first time the conception that nature had no history in time began to be shaken." (*Anti-Dühring*, p72)

Here Engels explains that previously the universe appeared to people only "as an incessant repetition of the same processes". After Kant, this could no longer be so easily asserted. For Engels, the birth and death of our solar system must for the same reason apply to all the solar systems in all the galaxies (or 'island universes' as Kant termed them). Engels repeats the idea briefly in *Ludwig Feuerbach and the Outcome of Classical German Philosophy* and develops it in greater detail in the introduction to *Dialectics of Nature.*

We should add that, before turning to philosophy, Kant participated in the dispute originally between Newton and Leibniz mentioned above, in a treatise defending Newton's concept of absolute space. Leibniz more correctly argued that space was relative. Engels says simply that Kant "didn't see clearly into the matter" (*Dialectics of Nature*, The measure of motion – Work, p118). As we have noted in the chapter, *Galileo and the relativity of space* (under the subhead *What is space?*), Engels correctly recognised that space is relative.

Hegel on the dialectics of infinity

Throughout his life, the German philosopher Hegel was an enthusiastic supporter of the French Revolution of 1789. Hegel, widely thought of as the most difficult of all philosophers to understand, followed in the radical philosophical tradition begun by Kant, who established a school of philosophy called *German Idealism*. Yet Hegel's idealist philosophy, and in particular his dialectics, when placed on a materialist basis by Karl Marx and Friedrich Engels, became one of the cornerstones of Marxism. Both Marx and Engels in their youth were Young Hegelians, radical opponents of the old autocracy of the German nation.

Engels comments that "the true significance and the revolutionary character of the Hegelian philosophy [was] that it once for all dealt the death blow to the finality of all products of human thought and action." Engels continues:

> *"Truth lay now in the process of cognition itself, in the long historical development of science, which mounts from lower to ever higher levels of knowledge without ever reaching, by discovering so-called absolute truth, a point at which it can proceed no further, where it would have nothing more to do than to fold its hands and gaze with wonder at the absolute truth to which it had attained."*
>
> Feuerbach and the End of Classical German Philosophy,
> in *Marx and Engels Selected Works*, p588

This alone should give Woods pause before stating, as a statement of absolute truth, that "Dialectical materialism conceives of the universe as infinite", and folding his hands, and gazing with wonder at the discoveries he has made.

There are more than a few respects in which, as Engels comments, the materialist outlook penetrated into Hegel's philosophy. "Hegel laboured to discover and demonstrate the pervading thread of development", and in doing so, "he played an epoch making role in every sphere". The forced constructions of Hegel's "system" are only the frame and scaffolding of his work, Engels says:

> *"If one does not loiter here needlessly, but presses on farther into the immense building, one finds innumerable treasures which today still possess undiminished value."*
> Feuerbach and the End of Classical German Philosophy, Selected Works, p590

Hegel on the 'potential' and 'actual' infinity of Aristotle

Hegel explicitly defends Aristotle's point of view on the infinite, that there is no "actual" infinity, only a potential infinity. Hegel says that: "The solutions propounded by Aristotle of these dialectical forms merit high praise". Hegel criticises the seventeenth century French philosopher, Pierre Bayle, who argued that "if matter is infinitely divisible, then it *actually* contains an infinite number of parts... [it is] an infinite that really and actually exists."(*Science of Logic*, p199, para 427)

"On the contrary", Hegel continues, this is only a "possibility, not an *existing* of the parts" (here Hegel substitutes the word "possibility" where Aristotle would use the word "potential").

Hegel says that Bayle commits the "error of holding mental fictions, such abstractions, as an infinite number of parts, to be something true and actual". (*Science of Logic*, p199, para 427)

Hegel and Newton's calculus

It appears that Woods is unfamiliar with what Hegel had to say on the infinite, although there are some seventy references to Hegel throughout *Reason in Revolt*. Hegel in general takes a position closer to materialism than Woods on this question; Woods is more idealist.

Hegel illuminates his views on the infinite by considering the following stanza of poetry by the eighteenth century German scientist and poet Albrecht von Haller.

> *"I heap up monstrous numbers,*
> *Pile millions upon millions,*
> *I put aeon upon aeon and world upon world,*
> *And when from that awful height*
> *Reeling, again I seek thee,*

All the might of number increased a thousandfold
Is still not a fragment of thee.
I remove them and thou liest wholly before me."

Quoted in *Science of Logic*, p230

Hegel remarks:

> "When this heaping and piling up of numbers is regarded as what
> is valuable in a description of eternity, it is overlooked that the poet
> himself declares this so-called terrifying journey into the beyond
> to be futile and empty.'

Hegel argues in various passages that it is futile and false to conceive of an infinite which exists somewhere "beyond". In his a *Science of Logic*, Hegel appears to reject the notion that the universe extends infinitely. Woods strives to make a complete distinction between the finite and the infinite, describing the infinite as, at first sight, "beyond all human experience", but Hegel rejects that separation.

Woods says:

> "The idea of the infinite seems difficult to grasp, because, at first sight,
> it is beyond all human experience... Mathematics deals with definite
> magnitudes. Infinity by its very nature cannot be counted or measured.
> This means there is a real conflict between the two. (p353)

But Hegel says:

> "Thus the infinite does not stand as something finished and complete
> above or superior to the finite, as if the finite had an enduring being
> apart from or subordinate to the infinite."

Science of Logic, p138

Yet Woods represents Hegel's outlook in the following way:

> "In the section on Quantity in the first volume of The Science of Logic,
> Hegel points out that, while the introduction of the mathematical
> infinite opened up new horizons for mathematics, and led to important
> results, it remained unexplained, because it clashed with the existing
> tradition and methods." (p355)

This is misleading. Firstly, one should start with the section *Infinity*, in the *Science of Logic*, if one wants to know Hegel's thoughts on the infinite directly. But Hegel is no less forthright in the section on *Quantity* to which Woods refers – the stanza of poetry above is from this section. Here Hegel examines Kant's antimony as to whether the world is finite or infinite. Woods mentions this antimony, and comments "It fell to the great dialectician Hegel to resolve the contradiction in *The Science of Logic.*" (p 146) So he did. But Woods fails to mention how Hegel resolves it. Hegel concludes his discussion with following reference to the dialectics of ancient Greece:

> *"But the so-called world… is never and nowhere without contradiction,*
> *but it is unable to endure it and is, therefore, subject to coming-to-be*
> *and ceasing-to-be.*
>
> Science of Logic, p238

Hegel, in other words, does not embrace a universe which is infinite in time and space in the Newtonian sense, but instead argues that the universe has a birth and a death. Nevertheless, it is true, as Woods infers, that in a remark on The Specific Nature of the Notion of the Mathematical Infinite, Hegel begins by recognising that the mathematical infinite led to "important results". (Science of Logic, p240) But let us be clear. Hegel here calls the infinities which mathematics uses, whether infinitely large or infinitely small, "pictorial conceptions which, when looked at more closely, turn out to be nebulous shadowy nullities". (Science of Logic, p238)

In calculus (which Hegel is discussing here), a series of numbers gets smaller, appearing to be an infinite series. But this series never reaches infinity. Instead, a new quality emerges from the result of the calculus. (*Science of Logic*, pp244-5) Hegel sees the dialectic at work here, where a new quality emerges from a quantitative process. For this reason, among others, Hegel praises the Newtonian method of calculus. (*Science of Logic*, p257) Hegel is normally in the habit of sharply criticising Newton in the *Science of Logic*.

Hegelian infinity: the negation of the negation

In his section *Infinity*, Hegel discusses the dialectic of a simple infinite series (a series where, for instance, you can always add one more to whatever number you arrive at). Each step in the series appears to be a step towards infinity, Hegel says, only to be negated, because this step takes you no nearer infinity at all. There is no point at which infinity is nearer, no matter how many numbers one counts, as the stanza of poetry which Hegel quotes demonstrates. Thus infinity can be said to be 'negated' by the finite.

But, yet, the counting has not stopped, and there is no conceivable point at which it will stop. So the finite is once again negated. In this way, Hegel introduces his famous "negation of the negation", because this second negation can be called the negation of the first negation, or the "negation of the negation". Once familiar, this concept is not complex. The finite is negated by the infinite, and then this negation of infinity is itself negated with the next finite step in the infinite series, which again raises the hope of achieving infinity. "The infinite is the negation of the negation", Hegel states. (*Science of Logic*, p137)

The infinite, concludes Hegel, always contains the finite within it, and is comprised of the finite:

> "*The finite reappears in the infinite itself as its other, because it is only in its connection with its other, the finite, that the infinite is.*"
>
> Science of Logic, p142

The infinite, Hegel says, again referring back to ancient Greece, is properly understood "essentially only as a becoming" (*Science of Logic*, p148), something that is in a process of further determination. Hegel's dialectic is a way of explaining why we consider, or can call, an infinite series 'infinite', although it never reaches infinity. Hegel emphasises that there is no "progress" towards infinity, since it is always negated and never gets nearer; there is only an infinite "process" which never leaves the finite.

Woods asks: "How can the universe be finite, and yet have no boundaries?" (p218) Hegel supplies the essence of the answer to this question, precisely one century before Einstein's general theory of relativity allowed that the curvature of space-time might cause the universe to curl round on itself: "the image of true infinity, bent back onto itself, becomes the circle." (*Science of Logic*, p149) To put it another way, the surface of any sphere is finite yet has no boundaries – an ant can crawl over a football forever, never coming to an end point, a boundary marking the end of the sphere.

Hegel and "bad infinity"

Woods says:

> "*In mathematics, it is possible to have an infinite series of numbers which starts with one. But, in practice, the idea of infinity cannot begin with one,*"

or any other number. Infinity is not a mathematical concept. It cannot be counted. This one-sided "infinity" is what Hegel calls bad infinity." (p218)

Hegel disparaged those who considered the infinite as something separate from the finite. The term "bad" infinity used by Woods has been replaced by the term "spurious" infinity in the modern translation of Hegel's *Science of Logic*. The Moscow (Progress Press, Lawrence and Wishart) translations of Engels' *Anti-Dühring* use the term "bad" infinity, but the highly regarded 1969 translation of Hegel's *Science of Logic* by A.V. Miller – marking the beginning of a revival of interest in Hegel – translates term to which Engels was referring as "spurious" rather than "bad".

It should be apparent from the foregoing discussion that Woods has misunderstood what Hegel believed. Hegel did not accept the actual existence of an infinity which exists apart from processes which can indeed be counted, whether mathematical or historical, except in his somewhat pantheistic concept of divinity.

While Woods argues that the finite and the infinite are qualitatively distinct, Hegel says:

> *"The infinite as thus posited over against the finite, in a relation wherein they are as qualitatively distinct others, is to be called the spurious infinite."*
>
> Science of Logic, p139

Hegel's spurious or bad infinity is the complete opposite of Woods' description of it, and it is precisely Hegel's spurious or bad infinity which Woods embraces – the infinity which cannot be counted, which stands apart from the finite, an infinite which "really and actually exists" as Bayle had said. Hegel says that: "such an infinite must be seen as a falsity". (*Science of Logic*, p149)

Hegel correctly associates this spurious infinity with the divine. When Woods repeats a favourite phrase of Ted Grant's, that the infinite universe contains "only galaxies and more galaxies stretching out to infinity", that is Hegel's bad infinity. Grant and Woods completely reverse the position that Hegel takes, and which Engels correctly champions.

Commenting on the Hubble telescope, the telescope which was launched into space and has captured many stunning images, Woods says:

> *"For our part, we welcome these epoch-making investigations, because they take the debate about the Big Bang out of the realm of abstract*

theorising and mathematical models, and into the field of practical observation ... We will predict now that they will see new surprises: not the Big Bang, but only galaxies and more galaxies stretching out to infinity."
Reason in Revolt, Preface to the 2001 Spanish edition, emphasis in original

The Big Bang had long been taken out of abstract theorising, while on the other hand, infinity will not be seen through the Hubble telescope. When astronomers turn their telescopes to view galaxies whose light has travelled to us over millions and billions of years, they are looking back in time in the sense that what they see actually took place millions or even billions of years ago, but its light has only just reached us. And what they see when they look back in time, in general, are galaxies in an earlier stage of formation and development. They see, for instance, galaxies in which the stars have not had time to manufacture as many of the elements that over millions and billions of years are products of the fusion process that powers the stars.

Woods omits to acknowledge that this is the overall picture. This process of the development of galaxies from the remnants of the Big Bang will be glanced at later. But what is not seen through telescopes is a mixture of older and younger galaxies irrespective of distance. There are no objects which challenge the widest range of ages given the universe, from ten to twenty billons years. The concept of an infinite universe containing "galaxies and more galaxies stretching out to infinity" is in conflict with the evidence, and has been for a very long time.

But only a year after his comments on the Hubble telescope in 2001, writing in the preface to the 2002 USA edition of *Reason in Revolt*, Woods endorsed a version of the 70-year-old cyclical Big Bang theory that interprets space as finite but time as infinite. Presumably, Woods was therefore prepared to accept the fallacy of the confident prediction of the previous year, of "only galaxies and more galaxies stretching out to infinity", a prediction which, after all, is not and cannot be based on practical observation at all, only on abstract theorising. However far one can see, one can never see infinity through a telescope.

The idealist philosopher Hegel supports the materialist view that infinity is an abstraction that is never realised, except, that is, in god – Hegel is still an idealist. Woods takes the idealist position, which Hegel calls "spurious" or "bad" infinity. It is an undialectical position, Hegel says:

"The falsification of the finite and infinite by the understanding which holds fast to a qualitatively distinct relation between them and asserts

that each in its own nature is separate from the other, comes from
forgetting what the Notion [dialectic] of these movements is."

Science of Logic, p145

Hegel has firmer dialectical reasons for rejecting the concept of a progression towards infinity. It is not just that infinity could never be reached or brought any nearer. For Hegel no apparently infinite process will go on indefinitely. Hegel understood that each additional quantity added to an infinite series could – and at some point in the concrete, material world, will – lead to a qualitative leap, and the whole process will be transformed into something else. Nothing stays the same. Everything comes into being and passes away. In the same way, those processes that we imagine could continue forever are mere figments of our imagination. When infinities appear in equations, physicists invariably work on the assumption that these infinities only mark out a point of qualitative transformation, or phase change. The idea of infinite space, stretching on without limit is undialectical because it is an idea of quantitative accumulation without a qualitative change.

Hegel explains that bad or spurious infinity "... is commonly held to be something sublime and a kind of divine worship". (*Science of Logic*, p228) He clearly considers Woods' approach undialectical:

> "*A second question in these metaphysical systems was: Is the world finite or infinite? The very terms of the question assume that the finite is a permanent contradictory [i.e. in permanent contradiction] to the infinite...*"

> "*Dogmatism consists in the tenacity which draws a hard and fast line between certain terms and others opposite to them. We may see this clearly in the strict 'either – or': for instance, The world is either finite or infinite; but one of these two it must be. The contrary of this rigidity is the characteristic of all [dialectical] truth.*"

Hegel, *Encyclopaedia*, paragraph 28 (remark), paragraph 32

We must, however, add a caveat. Engels explains that the Hegelian system presented itself in such a way that, in the final pages of his *Science of Logic*: "the whole dogmatic content of the Hegelian system is declared to be absolute truth, in contradiction to his dialectical method, which dissolves all dogmatism". (*Feuerbach and the End of Classical German Philosophy*, in *Marx and Engels Selected Works*, p589)

Hegel incorporated Kant's support for Newtonian absolute space (not to be confused with infinite space) into his philosophy. In the closing pages of *Science of Logic*, Hegel appears to mystically link absolute space and time with what he terms the *Absolute Idea*, a kind of mystical godhead.

Hegel writes that the Absolute Idea takes on the form of the "*externality of space and time* existing absolutely on its own account without the moment of subjectivity". (*Science of Logic*, p843) In a sense, Hegel is suggesting that once the Absolute Idea is reached in a great mystical cycle of the dialectical development of all things towards godhead, it returns, albeit at a higher level, to "nature", "the end being wound back into the beginning, the simple ground". (*Science of Logic*, pp842-3)

But this does not mean that Hegel endorses Newton's concept of an infinite universe. Space and time are absolute, in his view, but not infinite. Even in the closing paragraphs of *Science of Logic*, which contain an exposition of his dialectic – so that one might easily suppose that the "Absolute Idea" is nothing other than Hegel's dialectic – Hegel argues that the infinite is not in fixed opposition to the finite, as something "beyond".

Engels on materialism, the infinite and cosmology

Engels' materialism

"With each epoch-making discovery even in the sphere of natural science [materialism] has to change its form..."

Engels, *Ludwig Feuerbach and the Outcome of Classical German Philosophy, Selected Works*, p597

Since Einstein, quantum mechanics, and the Big Bang theory, materialism has to change its form. This means dialectical materialism too. We must remove old dogmas and begin again, starting from the recognition that the method of dialectical materialism at base is simply materialism represented dialectically.

Engels' statement also applies in a general sense to our former concepts of space, time and the infinite universe. But by contrast, Woods criticises specific scientific theories of space and time for departing from the Newtonian concept of time and space as embraced by Engels.

If it appeared to materialists in the 19th Century, albeit without evidence, that the world must be infinite, the epoch-making discoveries we will shortly discuss have forced a change. These discoveries may not be the final word, but there is no going back to the old dogmas, to the Newtonian outlook.

Dialectical materialism takes from Hegel its "death blow to the finality of all products of human thought and action" as Engels puts it. It is simply wrong, purely from a dialectical standpoint, let alone the current scientific standpoint, to state as if it were an incontrovertible fact that, "Dialectical materialism conceives of the universe as infinite" as Woods does. (p189)

Infinite space and time

It may be argued that Engels' works set into a kind of Marxist orthodoxy the Newtonian science of his time. In general, Engels was defending and exemplifying, quite correctly, a materialist approach to the world against those such as Eugen Dühring who were seeking to take the socialist movement back to an idealist, eclectic outlook. Engels necessarily proceeded on the basis of those current scientific ideas that appeared to be beyond question.

Woods, on the other hand, defends Engels' point of view not for its inherent respect for scientific validity, its materialism, but as if Engels was guided by some higher principle (to which Woods elevates dialectical materialism), which in some way lifted the Marxist method above that of scientific investigation.

He transforms Engels' viewpoint into dogma. Woods says *Reason in Revolt* defends "the fundamental ideas of the movement" in his 2006 obituary of Ted Grant (cited as co-author of *Reason in Revolt*). In truth, *Reason in Revolt* defends Engels' support for Newtonian physics somewhat as others defend the literal truth of *The Bible*, not as an expression of the Marxist method of historical materialism rooted in a particular epoch, a theoretical method that has to be continually re-evaluated as science advances our understanding of our world, but as a finished philosophical doctrine that literally serves for all time.

Engels' assumptions of infinite space and time in *Dialectics of Nature* should be considered in the light of his more detailed, systematic and repeated embracing of the Kantian theory of the origin of all existing celestial bodies (for example in *Anti-Dühring* and *Feuerbach*), which Engels, at one point called, "the theory of the origin of the universe" (*Dialectics of Nature*, p273), and his endorsement of Hegel's rejection of the spurious infinite.

These indicate a method, while Engels' assumption of infinite time and space merely represents the form, the science of the day. We should also keep in mind that most of *Dialectics of Nature* consists of unfinished and unrevised drafts and was abandoned unpublished in Engels' lifetime, although the introduction appears complete, and the fragment of the chapter entitled *Dialectics* is invaluable in demystifying Hegel's dialectics and making it accessible.

When Woods takes Engels as his authority for what he regards as dialectical materialism, it is doubly misleading, not just because it misrepresents Engels' methodology, but also because Engels does not make the crude mistakes that Woods does in relation to the concept of an infinite universe. When Engels discusses infinity in space and time in *Anti-Dühring*, he talks about a "process" which is "unrolling" in the context of an infinity which is "composed of nothing but finites".

Singularities, "Bad" infinity, and the beginning of the universe

Engels writes:

"For that matter, Herr Dühring will never succeed in conceiving real infinity without contradiction. Infinity is a contradiction, and is full of contradictions. From the outset it is a contradiction that an infinity is composed of nothing but finites, and yet this is the case."

Engels reflects Hegel's dialectic of the infinite – that the infinite is comprised of nothing but finites, for which concept Hegel himself credits Aristotle. Woods misrepresents Engels, turning his position upside down, when discussing Hegel's "bad" infinity. For those for whom this may be a matter of some contention, it is worth a moments' discussion. (In the chapter, *Hegel on the dialectics of infinity*, we mentioned that what Engels terms Hegel's "bad" infinity, in the Moscow translation of *Anti-Dühring*, is a translation of what in the Miller edition of Hegel's *Science of Logic* is termed the "spurious" infinite. We discussed what Hegel meant by the term.)

In the course of his criticism of Herr Dühring, Engels says that:

"Infinity – which Hegel calls bad infinity – is attributed to being, also in accordance with Hegel (Encyclopaedia, § 93), and then this infinity is investigated."

Anti-Dühring, p61

What is perhaps self-evident to Engels and his contemporaries in the above statement, but less than evident to his modern reader, is that when Engels says that "bad" infinity is "attributed to being" in the above quote, he here refers in particular to Dühring's concept of the primordial beginning of the universe, discussed in his section on 'World Schematism'. This is a concept which Dühring had plagiarised from Hegel, and which both termed "Being".

When Hegel appears to describe the world coming into being, at the very beginning of his *Science of Logic*, he begins with: "Being, pure being, without any further determination". Hegel later defines this undifferentiated pure being from which the rest of the world appears to emerge as "infinite being", which appears to be a type of pantheistic godhead. (*Science of Logic*, p100, § 164)

The reader might wonder how Hegel's beginning of the world in this "undifferentiated pure being" compares to the well known theory, based on the research done by Stephen Hawking and Roger Penrose in 1970, which suggests that the universe emerged from a "singularity". But the concept of a singularity, although widely accepted for a time, is no longer part of the standard model of the Big Bang. One reason for this is that there is insufficient observational evidence, but another is that the theory of singularities is plagued with infinities, and scientists are usually averse to infinities which arise in theories, treating them as errors in the equations or an indication of a false theory. The standard Big Bang theory is based on well established evidence for a hot dense origin to the universe, by extrapolating the observed universe back in time, but it cannot extrapolate back as far as a singularity. Hawking himself went on to study the possibility that quantum mechanical effects would operate at very small sizes, so that no singularity would arise. Strangely, Woods considers singularities "extremely unlikely", despite the fact that if a singularity existed which had achieved infinite density it might be considered proof of the existence of something which was infinite.

Engels takes pleasure in showing that the anti-Marxist Dühring has plagiarised Hegel, including his concept of the world beginning with an undifferentiated essence. But here is the difference. In the idealist Hegel's system, this undifferentiated being is subject to a somewhat vague dialectical process, and develops into a more "determinate" being – that is, develops into the world as we know it. Hegel feels no compelling need for materialist causes to achieve this (and is, at any rate, working on many levels, least of all the physical.)

But Dühring takes at face value Hegel's primordial "being" and then removes the dialectical concept from it. Dühring is scathingly critical of Hegel and castigates his dialectics. Dühring purports to embrace materialism, and has supposedly disproved the existence of God already – albeit, Engels points out ironically, using proofs not dissimilar to those specious proofs that past philosophers used to prove the existence of God. But without any support from Hegel's idealist dialectics, Dühring is deprived of any means to enable his second-hand unchanging undifferentiated being to change into the world as we know it, since he has said it is unchanging.

Herr Dühring's universe really starts with a being which lacks all inner differentiation, all motion and change" Engels says, and quotes Dühring:

> "...all periodical processes of nature must have had some beginning, and all differentiation, all the multifariousness of nature which appears in succession must have its roots in one self-equal state. This state may, without involving a contradiction, have existed from eternity... "

> *Anti-Dühring*, p58 and p62

So here we have Dühring's "bad" infinity – an actually existing infinity – an eternity of unchanging, undialectical existence of a "self-equal state" before the world came into being. Scientists today suppose there must be a substratum from which the Big Bang origin of the universe emerged, but current theories picture a very dynamic terrain. Dühring claims that the origin of the universe is an actual, eternally existing "self-equal state" or being. Hegel calls concepts such as the idea of infinity as an actually existing thing, the "spurious infinite", which Engels translates as "bad" infinity. The one exception Hegel makes to the "spurious infinite" is the same exception that Aristotle makes, as we have explained – the divine. Hegel's mysterious godhead is "infinite being".

Engels gleefully points out the contradictions which Dühring has got himself into by plagiarising Hegel, and, as we have seen, gives a reference to Hegel's Encyclopaedia: "Infinity – which Hegel calls bad infinity – is attributed to being, also in accordance with Hegel (*Encyclopaedia*, § 93), and then this infinity is investigated." Dühring has painted himself into a tight spot. Engels refers the reader to paragraph 93 of Hegel's *Encyclopaedia* (quoted below) and proceeds to show, with great delight, that Dühring's investigation of the infinite is also plagiarised – this time from Kant.

Engels proceeds to remonstrate with Dühring's notion that there can exist, "the counted infinite numerical series". He challenges Dühring to do the "clever trick of counting it". This again invokes Hegel's spurious or bad infinity, because by a "counted" infinite series Dühring intends to indicate a finished, completed, existing infinity, a progress to infinity which is completed with the capturing, so to speak, of an actual, "counted" infinity. This is not the infinite process of counting, which is comprised only of finites. Engels can see how Dühring slips between acceptable notions of an infinite series and the bad or spurious infinity of an actually existing "self-equal state".

The distinction, however, is subtle. Engels attacks the inconsistencies and vagaries in Dühring's verbal gyrations around concepts of an infinite series, and these attacks could easily be mistaken for attacks on the concept of an infinite series as such, and this is what Woods does. Nevertheless, two paragraphs later, Engels plainly states that infinity is a contradiction and is "composed of nothing but finites".

It is in these paragraphs – to add further confusion – that Engels makes a clear assertion of infinite space and time. He does so because that was the overwhelmingly accepted scientific conception of the period, and he keeps his dialectical insights in check where physical evidence is lacking. But Engels does not hesitate to call attention to the passage in Hegel's

Encyclopaedia where he calls infinite space a "barren declamation", and modern science would tend to agree.

In his *Encyclopaedia*, paragraph § 93, Hegel briefly refers to the false concept of a progression towards infinity, as opposed to a process which can be infinitely repeated but which gets no nearer to infinity. He then says:

> *"When time and space, for example, are spoken of as infinite, it is in the first place the infinite progression on which our thoughts fasten. We say, Now, This time, and then we keep continually going forwards and backwards beyond this limit. The case is the same with space, the infinity of which has formed the theme of barren declamation to astronomers with a talent for edification."*

> *"In the attempt to contemplate such an infinite, our thought, we are commonly informed, must sink exhausted. It is true indeed that we must abandon the unending contemplation, not however because the occupation is too sublime, but because it is too tedious. It is tedious to expatiate in the contemplation of this infinite progression, because the same thing is constantly recurring. We lay down a limit: then we pass it: next we have a limit once more, and so on for ever. All this is but superficial alternation, which never leaves the region of the finite behind. To suppose that by stepping out and away into that infinity we release ourselves from the finite, is in truth but to seek the release which comes by flight. But the man who flees is not yet free: in fleeing he is still conditioned by that from which he flees."*

> *"If it be also said that the infinite is unattainable, the statement is true, but only because to the idea of infinity has been attached the circumstance of being simply and solely negative. With such empty and other-world stuff philosophy has nothing to do. What philosophy has to do with is always something concrete and in the highest sense present."*
>
> *Encyclopaedia*, para 94

Hegel returns us to the concrete from false notions of an infinite progression through space and time. Hegel applies the term "spurious" or "bad" infinity not only to a notion that an infinity of space actually exists, but also to the supposedly "sublime" descriptions of a "progress" to infinity through a tedious repetition, for instance of galaxies beyond galaxies stretching to infinity. His point is that there is no such thing as an independently existing infinity and one does not make any progress towards it.

It is remarkable that Woods missed this since Engels specifically refers to it at the beginning of the chapter from which Woods quotes. In fact, Woods twice uses the same large quote from Engels to back up his assertions about his notion of infinity. (p218 and p358) But he twice stops short of the paragraph which immediately follows and casts an entirely new light on what preceded it:

"For that matter, Herr Dühring will never succeed in conceiving real infinity without contradiction. Infinity is a contradiction, and is full of contradictions. From the outset it is a contradiction that an infinity is composed of nothing but finites, and yet this is the case."

"The limitedness of the material world leads no less to contradictions than its unlimitedness, and every attempt to get over these contradictions leads, as we have seen, to new and worse contradictions. It is just because infinity is a contradiction that it is an infinite process, unrolling endlessly in time and in space. The removal of the contradiction would be the end of infinity. Hegel saw this quite correctly, and for that reason treated with well-merited contempt the gentlemen who subtilised over this contradiction."

Anti-Dühring, Part V, p66

Here Engels refines his support for infinite space and time with Hegel's concept of the infinite (as being comprised of nothing but finites) clearly in mind. This passage bears some, slightly forced, comparison with modern science, which currently calculates that the universe will expand indefinitely – an infinite process, unrolling endlessly.

Cosmology

For Engels, the "Kantian theory of the origin of all existing celestial bodies", which we discussed in the chapter, *Kant's cosmology and Engels' commentary*, means not just that the galaxies of our universe have a history in time, coming into being at some definite time in the past, but also that they will pass away. "Nature," Engels emphasises, "does not just exist, but *comes into being* and *passes away*." And he discusses exactly this passing away, basing himself on some scientific speculation of the period.

"Nevertheless, 'all that comes into being deserves to perish'... instead of the bright, warm solar system with its harmonious arrangement of

members, only a cold, dead sphere will still pursue its lonely path through universal space. And what will happen to our solar system will happen sooner or later to all the other systems of our island universe; it will happen to all the other innumerable island universes, even to those the light of which will never reach the earth while there is a living human eye to receive it.

"And when such a solar system has completed its life history and succumbs to the fate of all that is finite, death, what then?"

Later, Engels adds:

"The view is being arrived at that heavenly bodies are ultimately destined to fall into one another... so that all motion in general will have ceased."
Dialectics of Nature, p38, p50-2

Surely, all this demonstrates that Engels would have expressed little surprise if told that our universe was discovered to have a history in time – a birth perhaps ten to twenty billion years ago? Surely he would say that Kant predicted it centuries ago?

In fact, in note form, he did: "Kant – the theory of the origin of the universe before Laplace". (*Dialectics of Nature*, p273) Engels emphasises "*before*" because the work of Laplace provided a proof of Kant's insight, at least in relation to the development of solar systems, now typically termed the Kant-Laplace nebular hypothesis. This note appears in the fragment headed "Büchner", which is thought to be the first fragment or set of notes which Engels made for the composition of *Dialectics of Nature*, written in 1873.

But Engels has more to say on the matter. One must allow for some naturally out-dated science and scientific terminology, such as the use of the term "motion", which was the very latest terminology at the time but was shortly to be superseded by the term "energy". We also remember the fact that Engels predates Einstein and Hubble, both of whom gave a much more definite material meaning to time and space, matter and energy, so that they can only arise together. Making this reasonable allowance, Engels would not encounter many objections from modern scientists in seeking a substratum from which our universe emerged:

"This much is certain: there was a time when the matter of our island universe had transformed a quantity of motion [i.e. energy] - of what kind we do not yet know - into heat, such that there could be developed

from it the solar systems appertaining to (according to Mädler) at least twenty million stars, the gradual extinction of which is likewise certain. How did this transformation take place? We know just as little as [the astro-physicist] Father Secchi knows whether the future caput mortuum of our solar system will once again be converted into the raw material of a new solar system. But here either we must have recourse to a creator, or we are forced to the conclusion that the incandescent raw material for the solar system of our universe was produced in a natural way by transformations of motion which are by nature inherent in moving matter, and the conditions of which therefore also must be reproduced by matter, even if only after millions and millions of years and more or less by chance but with the necessity that is also inherent in chance."

Dialectics of Nature, p51

Leaving aside the exact terminology of 'matter' and 'motion', most scientists would not deny the main thrust behind such speculation, which is that whatever substratum gave rise to our universe, the processes are natural and are likely to reoccur. The difference is that scientists today do not take for granted that any newly emerging universe needs to have the same physical constants, so that it may not be comprised of energy, matter, space and time in the same way that our universe is.

Does Engels' approach not show that Woods' scheme has no history in time? That there we find just an endless repetition: "only galaxies and more galaxies stretching out to infinity"?

And does not Engels also see that there are processes going on inside these stars? That they and the galaxies they inhabit are consuming and changing their elemental constituent atoms, so that they must have a history in time? This history is written in the current make-up of the elements (for instance hydrogen, helium, oxygen, carbon, nitrogen, silicon, calcium, and iron) found in stars, which can be detected in their light. It tells us whether they are first generation stars, or stars that are consuming in part the remnants of a previous generation of stars. Observation can in practice tell how old galaxies are. How could an infinite universe be a never-ending replication of our current state - galaxies stretching to infinity? Would this not be a rather static viewpoint?

Woods poses a challenge, which might as well be directed at Engels: "The problem is: how to get from nothing to something? If one is religiously minded, there is no problem; God created the universe from nothing." (p210)

In his notes, Engels quotes Angelo Secchi without comment:

"Secchi (p 810) himself asks: When the sun and the whole system are extinct, "are there forces in nature which can reconvert the dead system into its original state of glowing nebula and reawaken it to new life? We do not know."

Dialectics of Nature, p367, quoting from Secchi's book *Die Sonne*

Engels' reply in general terms is the same reply that modern science and materialist scientists generally give: "we do not know", although there are many interesting possibilities. (Undoubtedly, there are some scientists who, despite investigating materialist reality, hold religious beliefs and in some cases support 'creationist' theories.) But Woods forgets that coming in to being and passing away is one of the fundamental laws of dialectics. From what substratum, we do not know, but "Nature," says Engels, "does not just exist, but comes into being and passes away." (*Dialectics of Nature*, p38) From a purely dialectical point of view, this presents no problems.

Engels shows that dialectical materialism refuses to "conceive of the universe as infinite" except perhaps as an infinite process which is composed of the finite and, perhaps, is comprised of universes which come into being and will have an end.

But as for a cyclical universe, such as the theory that Woods endorsed in 2002, the infinite repetition of Big Bangs, Engels refutes it in advance – its authors, Steinhardt and Turok, now recognise their mistake here – when he says that:

"... in the last resort, Nature works dialectically and not metaphysically; that she does not move in the eternal oneness of a perpetually recurring circle, but goes through a real historical evolution."

Socialism, Utopian and Scientific, Selected Works, p407

The infinite in mathematics

I n the late nineteenth century the mathematician George Cantor dedicated his studies to the mathematical concepts of the infinite. Woods says:

"Thus, after Cantor, there can be no argument about the central place of the infinite in mathematics… Yet despite all the evidence, many modern mathematicians persist in denying the objectivity of infinity." (p358)

How can this perversity of modern mathematics be resolved? Why, if there was to be no argument about the objective existence of infinity, did argument persist "despite all the evidence"? The answer is to be found in discovering what Cantor actually showed. Cantor says that the infinite arises:

"First when it is realised in the most complete form, in a fully independent other-worldly being, in Deo [in god] where I call it the Absolute… second when it occurs in the contingent, created world; third… as a mathematical magnitude…"

"I wish to make a sharp contrast between the Absolute and the transfinite, that is the actual infinities of the last two sorts, which are clearly limited, subject to further increase, and thus related to the finite."

Quoted by Barrow, *The Infinite Book*, p94

In Cantor's mathematics, only infinity in god coincides with Woods' idea of the objectivity of infinity – an objectively existing infinite god. And indeed there was "no argument" about it.

Einstein and the end of Newtonian absolute space and time

By the end of the nineteenth century scientists were faced with a contradiction in physics that seemed to throw into question all of Newtonian physics, including Newton's first law of motion, based on Galileo's principle of relativity.

It was Einstein who successfully resolved these contradictions into an entirely new physics at the turn of the twentieth century, later laying the basis for an entirely new cosmology.

One of the great questions of the late nineteenth century was what medium light waves travelled through. Termed aether, this medium was thought to be an absolute frame of reference, a medium that was stationary with respect to the universe. A large number of experiments were conducted to try to detect it.

Scientists thought that, if light was transmitted through the aether at a definite speed, as the earth moved in its elliptical orbit through the same medium, the speed of light from a particular source should appear to vary over the course of twelve months.

For instance, imagine a distant star that the earth happens to travel first towards and then away from as it orbits the sun each year. As the earth travels towards the

Albert Einstein (1879–1955) was a socialist and an opponent of nuclear armaments

star, meeting the starlight from the star, Newtonian physics supposes that the starlight will appear to be travelling faster than six months later, when the earth's orbit takes it speeding away from the same starlight.

The same measurement conducted as the earth rushed away from the starlight should find the speed of light to be slower, because the star light was catching up the earth – like the difference between a head-on collision and a bump from behind. The car speeds may be the same but the consequences of a head on collision are far worse. Newton's theory suggests a difference of roughly sixty kilometres per second between these two measurements.

In 1887 Albert Michelson and Edward Morley conducted a famous experiment to detect the aether. But they failed to measure any difference in the speed of light travelling from any direction, irrespective of the motion of its source. Their 'null result' was shocking and unexpected. The aether did not appear to exist but, more importantly, the experiment confirmed what James Clerk Maxwell's theories seemed to suggest: that light propagated at the same speed irrespective of any motion, either of the source or the measuring device.

Light appeared to break Galileo's principle of relativity. It refused to obey Newtonian physics. The speed of light is invariant regardless of the motion of the observer or the light emitting source – for instance, light does not appear to us to go faster if it emerges from a star moving rapidly towards us or slower from a star receding from us. Light from a star is *red-shifted* if a star is moving away from us, and *blue-shifted* if it is moving towards us, because the wavelength of the light is lengthened towards the red end of the spectrum or shortened towards the blue. The length of the light waves change, but the speed that the waves travel through space remains the same. The speed of light is not relative to the motion of any frame of reference. Light always appears to be going at the same speed to all observers – that is to say, to all measuring devices, all frames of reference.

The experiment, and many others like it since, established as objective fact this peculiarity of the motion of light, which simply did not fit in to the seemingly orderly and common sense Newtonian view of the world. Needless to say, Woods does not recognise this seminal failure of Newtonian physics.

As a result of many experimental results, but particularly the 1887 Michelson and Morley experiment which was far more accurate than any made before, Einstein commented:

> *"Prominent theoretical physicists were therefore more inclined to reject [Galileo's] principle of relativity, despite the fact that no empirical data had been found that were contradictory to this principle."*
>
> Relativity, p19

In 1903 the physicist Hendrik Lorenz produced an equation, termed the *Lorenz transformation*, which offered a mathematical expression for measuring motion based on the results of the Michelson-Morley experiment, taking this aberrant behaviour of light as its basis. The unusual result of this equation was that length shortens in the direction of motion and time slows too – a result Lorenz was not at all happy about. Einstein adopted the Lorenz transformation, but rejected the undetectable aether, for which there was no evidence.

By 1905, Einstein had pieced together the *theory of relativity*, which could explain the null result of Michelson-Morley. He was able to derive the Lorenz transformation equation directly from considerations based on rejecting two false assumptions made by Newtonian physics in relation to Galileo's principle of relativity. For Newtonian science, motion was relative, but the motion of objects took place on a stage which was assumed to be comprised of absolute space and time. Einstein re-examined Galileo's principle of relativity, and removed these assumptions.

Let us return to the train and the pedestrian of Einstein's popular exposition of relativity, written in 1916. The train is one frame of reference, which is moving with respect to the other, the footpath on the embankment, where a pedestrian watches a stone fall from a window of the train.

We must note again in passing – what should by now be obvious to the reader – that the notion of an 'observer' (the pedestrian in this case), is a common technique, particularly but not exclusively used in popular scientific literature to communicate in accessible form the physics which, in scientific terms, may be expressed by a measurement taken from the stated system of coordinates (frame of reference), and so forth. There is no requirement for an actual observer – the truth of both Galileo's results and those of Einstein remain valid even if no human being ever walked the earth. It is not necessary for Woods to sarcastically object: "Presumably, if there is no observer, there is no time!" (p215) The presumption is wrong and absurd.

Einstein's considerations described here never wander from the objective to the subjective, from experimental evidence to speculative philosophy. Rather the opposite. This may be confirmed by examining Einstein's original 1905 paper, *On The Electrodynamics Of Moving Bodies* (which proposed the theory which became known as the special theory of relativity) at http://www.fourmilab.ch/etexts/einstein/specrel/www even though Einstein makes use of the term "the observer" in the relatively accessible opening paragraphs.

Let us return to Einstein's popular exposition. The passenger on the train drops a stone. Einstein points out that the train passenger and the pedestrian do not see the stone falling simultaneously. Here is the oversight of Galileo-Newtonian physics, inevitable in their day. Light must travel from the stone to the observers (or measuring instruments). Furthermore, the Michelson-Morley experiment had confirmed the peculiar nature of light's propagation between the two frames of reference – the speed of light is constant and is not affected by the fact that the train is in motion.

Let us spend two paragraphs giving a slightly more detailed exposition of this question. In *The Elegant Universe*, Brian Greene provides an excellent example of Einstein's crucial critique of Newtonian physics' assumption of simultaneity, which reduces itself to this: imagine a light is switched on in the middle of a carriage of the train, at an equal distance between two passengers at either end of the carriage, one at the front, and one at the rear. The light strikes both passengers simultaneously, as measured by atomic clocks in the carriage, since the train carriage is their stationary frame of reference and light has an equal distance to travel. But the train is moving as viewed from the platform. Viewed or measured from the platform, the light appears to strike the passenger at the rear of the carriage first, because from the point of view of the platform, he is moving forwards towards the light.

Here is where the strange properties of light come in. Measured from the platform, the light has further to go to reach the passenger at the front of the carriage since the train is moving, again as measured from the frame of reference of the platform. And the speed of light remains constant no matter which frame of reference you are in. Since the passenger at the front of the train has travelled further from the light, and the passenger at the rear has travelled towards the light, the distances the light has to travel, from the point of view of the platform, are different, and so it strikes the two passengers at different times. Simultaneous events in time in one frame of reference (the train) are not simultaneous with respect to a different frame of reference (the platform). Time and space are different on the moving train, as observed from the platform.

Newtonian assumption of absolute time exposed

After discussing this, in a key passage in his popular exposition of relativity, Einstein comments:

"Now before the advent of theory of relativity it had always been tacitly assumed in physics that the statement of time had an absolute significance, i.e. that it is independent of the state of motion of the body of reference. But we have just seen that this assumption is incompatible with the most natural definition of simultaneity; if we discard this assumption, then the conflict between the law of propagation of light in vacuo [in a vacuum] and [Galileo's] principle of relativity disappears."

Relativity, p27

The assumption of Newtonian physics that "time had an absolute significance", which Einstein exposes as a false assumption, is precisely that which Woods ardently defends.

Woods attacks "the subjectivist interpretation of time, which makes it dependent on ('relative to') an observer. But time is an objective phenomenon, which is independent of any observer." (p215) This muddled position consists firstly of an attack on a 'straw man': a misrepresentation of Einstein's relativity as a form of subjective idealism – a misunderstanding which was all too common among popular commentators in the first half of the last century. Secondly, Woods' comments are also a clear defence of absolute time, which has no material basis. *Reason in Revolt* is mired in a swamp of such mistakes and misapprehensions.

Time is objective, of course, but has no meaning independent of a specific frame of reference. The modern scientific concept of time is not the "product of a definite philosophical point of view, smuggled in under the banner of 'relativity theory'." (p215) Rather, the idea of absolute time is an ideal which originates with Newton's belief in god, and which was hidden in the preconceptions of the measurement of motion dating back to René Descartes. Woods is incorrect to continue: "You see, for time to be 'real', it

Table 4: Schematic summary of Einstein's outlook added to *Table 3*

	Motion		Universe		Infinity
	Space	**Time**	**Space**	**Time**	
Aristotle	Absolute	Absolute	Finite	Ininite	Denied actual infinite
	Denied the existence of space and time outside the sphere of the universe				
Galileo	Relative	Relative	Finite (assumed)	Infinite (assumed)	Showed paradoxes of infinite
Newton	Absolute	Absolute	Ininite	Ininite	God as Infinite
	Laws of motion based on relative space & time; assumed absolute space & time real but undetected				
Einstein	Relative	Relative	'Only two things are infinite, the universe and human stupidity, and I'm not sure about the former' (attributed to Einstein). Einstein eventually came to accept a finite universe.		

needs an observer, who can then interpret it from his or her point of view." This has no bearing on relativity, and in any case bears no relation to the viewpoint of science of the last four centuries. It is a complete misunderstanding of scientific shorthand.

Einstein showed that between the two frames of reference, the train and the embankment, the Lorenz transformation provided a set of equations that could relate them objectively to one another so that one could express the motion of the stone falling from the train as viewed from the embankment – in long-hand, as measured according to the frame of reference of the embankment – in a way consistent with all known physical observations, but with astonishing results.

In essence, Einstein began by returning to Galileo's principle of relativity, but stripped of the idealist notions of time that Woods embraces. Then he entered into the equations the newly discovered enigmatic properties of the constant speed of light. The result was a new theoretical understanding of the physical nature of time and space.

While many aspects of Einstein's special theory of relativity were soon proven, it was thirty-six years before the first experiment (1941) that measured 'time dilation', and sixty-six years before the definitive experiment (1971) which we discussed in the chapter, *Galileo and the relativity of space*. Einstein had shown that time on a moving train passes more slowly than time on the embankment, just as the Lorenz transformation seemed to imply. Einstein can assert that when measured from the embankment, "as a consequence of its motion the clock goes more slowly than at rest." (Einstein, *Relativity*, p37)

The difference in the times measured in each case is so small that only if the motion of the train and clock was near to the speed of light would it be noticeable, without the aid of atomic clocks. This theory, along with the general theory of relativity, was proven experimentally in 1971 using atomic clocks on a passenger airplane. Further, the moving train appears to shorten slightly, as viewed from the embankment, since it was "shorter when in motion than at rest, and the more quickly it is moving, the shorter" it gets. (Einstein, *Relativity*, p35) Again, this shortening is completely beyond our experience (and so inevitably strikes us at first as a little absurd), since the train at normal speeds would shorten very considerably less than the width of an atom.

Einstein's theory of relativity could reconcile all experimentally proven aspects of reality. Indeed, other forgotten anomalies (or contradictions) which could not be explained by Newtonian concepts of absolute space and time, such as the anomalous path of the planet Mercury, were resolved by Einstein's general theory of relativity which, as Woods admits, predicted Mercury's path far more precisely on the basis of the new understanding of the warping of space-time.

The science of the atom bomb

The Lorenz transformation, adopted by Einstein, included the peculiar properties of light discovered by the Michelson-Morley experiment. In consequence, the speed of light, denoted by 'c' (or more precisely, the speed of light squared, c^2), appears in Einstein's equations.

Einstein followed his 1905 paper, which introduced special relativity, with a short paper in the same year that showed a formula could be derived from the equations of special relativity: the famous $e = mc^2$ – "energy equals mass multiplied by the speed of light squared".

Since the speed of light is determined by a distance in space over a certain time, the equation shows the complete link between energy, mass and space and time. Breathtakingly, Greene emphasises:

> "The combined speed of any object's motion through space and its motion through time is always precisely equal to the speed of light."
> The Fabric of the Cosmos, p49

Woods correctly endorses Einstein's $e = mc^2$, but without understanding its derivation or implication.

> "To common sense the mass of an object never changes... Later this law was found to be incorrect. It was found that mass increases with velocity... The predictions of special relativity have been shown to correspond to the observed facts." (p152)

Woods cannot avoid endorsing the formula that explains and gave rise to the atom bomb.

Motion through space-time affects mass-energy. The two are inextricably linked. Space and time, mass and energy, in our universe become an integral whole. It seems to follow that if the mass and energy of our universe have an origin, so does space-time, and one arrives back (on a higher level) at Aristotle's discussion of the origins of the universe. For Aristotle, outside of the universe – where there is nothing, no universe, as reference – there is no space and time. And if the heavens are corruptible, and have come into being and will pass away, so will the space-time of our universe. (This is not to speak of causes, of a substratum from which the universe arose, but of the relationship between space-time and mass-energy in our existing universe.) Of course, Aristotle, as we have said, thought that the heavens were unchanging and not corruptible.

But Woods cannot accept that time is relative to the observer, nor understand that this is an objective, not a subjective, fact of life, an aspect, for instance, of the everyday use of satellite navigational aids. He writes:

"The question is whether the laws of nature, including time, are the same for everyone, regardless of the place in which they are and the speed at which they are moving. On this question, Einstein vacillated. At times, he seemed to accept it, but elsewhere he rejected it."

And

"Einstein, under the influence of Ernst Mach, treated time as something subjective, which depended on the observer, at least in the beginning..." *(p168)*

Neither statement is true.

Woods pours scorn on the application of Einstein's relativity in modern science, calling it "subjective idealism".

"[The] empty abstraction Time, envisaged as an independent entity which is born and dies, and generally gets up to all kinds of tricks, along with its friend, Space, which arises and collapses and bends, a bit like a cosmic drunkard, and ends up swallowing hapless astronauts in black holes." *(p216)*

But this satire rebounds on Woods. He appears to contradict himself. He endorses $e = mc^2$ despite the fact that it is derived from a theory that he rejects and ridicules. Woods asserts that "mass increases with velocity" yet rejects the concept of the relativity of space and time which underlies this discovery. Woods appears to be unaware of the physics. The careful reader of *Reason in Revolt* will discern that Woods sometimes attributes the relativity of time to Einstein's later general theory of relativity, which he denigrates, and does not recognise that it is integral to Einstein's special relativity, which Woods associates with the formula $e = mc^2$.

The Big Bang and mysticism in science

Woods claims that, "At no time in the history of science has mysticism been so rampant as now." (p384) He darkly asserts that "determined attempts" are being made to "drag science backwards" (p381) and that the supposed subjectivism in Einstein's relativity "beyond doubt, exercised the most harmful influence upon modern science". (p167) "To blur the distinction between science and mysticism is to put the clock back 400 years," he warns. (p199) Woods argues that the temple shrine in this citadel of mysticism is the Big Bang theory.

Has science been set back 400 years? These are absurd claims. Most scientists are not practising mystics but in many respects salaried workers, of whose work Woods approves and disapproves arbitrarily. "Fortunately," says Woods, "it is possible to work out quite accurately the amount of matter in the observable universe. It is about one atom for every ten cubic metre of space." (p191)

How is it possible? Who did the science? Who should be credited? Why give merit to this cosmological observation and yet deride current cosmology as a whole? The reliability of such results are interdependent on the current state of cosmological theories in general – estimates of the number of atoms in the universe is not some isolated Herculean counting exercise carried out by an unknown, but an integral part of the current theories of the universe. Yet Woods rejects this general cosmological framework, which he says is "frequently bordering on mysticism". (p183)

The Big Bang

What are Woods' objections to the science of the Big Bang itself? The Big Bang theory rests on four pillars of evidence. This is how the University of Cambridge's cosmology website outlines them:

1. *Expansion of the universe*
2. *Origin of the cosmic background radiation*
3. *Nucleosynthesis of the light elements*

4. Formation of galaxies and large-scale structure
http://www.damtp.cam.ac.uk/user/gr/public/bb_pillars.html

The Big Bang theory is the only theory which provides a consistent explana-tion for the observed universe: firstly, of course, its expansion, and second-ly, the ancient cosmic background radiation, to which we will return.

Thirdly, it explains why there existed light elements, mainly hydrogen and helium, before there were any stars in our universe. Stars formed from these light elements. The processes which take place during the life and death of stars produces all the other elements which go to make up the chemistry of the universe (the elements of the periodic table, such as oxygen, carbon, silicon, iron, calcium, and so on). But they do not manufacture hydrogen, they only consume it, and the quantity of helium produced by a star is less than it consumes.

Fourthly, alongside a full account of the relative abundance of the light elements that make up the universe, the Big Bang theory is able to account in general terms for the formation of galaxies and other large-scale structures of the universe.

The Big Bang therefore for the first time gives the universe a history in time. It further elegantly solved the centuries-old paradoxes that had puzzled scientists, such as that of the universe collapsing in on itself through gravitational attraction, and Olbers' paradox, which we discussed in the chapter, *Newton: belief and contradiction*. It accurately predicts the abundance of elements: why there is so much hydrogen, created together with helium in the Big Bang, and the current proportion of the heavier atoms, created in the stars during the period since the Big Bang. (The calculation of the abundance of these elements has even more credibility because they were first made by a team led by Fred Hoyle, an opponent of the Big Bang theory.)

However, the piece of evidence that brought the Big Bang theory into mainstream cosmology was the accidental discovery of the last distant echoes of the Big Bang epoch: the cosmic background radiation.

The cosmic background radiation discovery

Woods objects that Big Bang theorists "move the goalposts" (p222), continually shifting the theories associated with the Big Bang universe around to fit the latest sets of data. It is true that experimental data often provides unpleasant surprises for researchers, and that theories have to be re-examined in the light of new discoveries. But Woods argues that this continual readjustment of theory in the light of new facts shows that the Big Bang theory is not science, but mysticism. In this, Woods follows Eric J Lerner, author of *The Big Bang Never Happened*, who is well known for his attacks on the Big Bang 'orthodoxy'. Lerner's tribute to the remarkable scientist Hannes Alfven is reproduced by permission on the opening pages of *Reason in Revolt* (but omitted in the second edition), and he is quoted as an authority throughout, particularly in the chapter on the Big Bang.

Lerner believes that the scientific establishment bureaucratically defends orthodox theories to the exclusion of competing theories. This is an important point but Lerner views it in an entirely one-sided manner. It is ironic that the Big Bang theory is precisely one that was derided fifty years ago, but has become a mainstream theory, perhaps in particular as a result of the discovery of the cosmic background radiation.

Lerner and Woods make out that the bias in science towards the established orthodoxy is a shocking new phenomenon. But it has always been so. As the philosopher Thomas Kuhn remarked in *The Structure of Scientific Revolutions*, the establishment of paradigms (Aristotle's universe, Newton's universe, Einstein's universe, the Big Bang universe) directs research to a particular ground, so to speak, establishing what then becomes normal science.

In the field of astronomy, Kuhn adds, the establishment of paradigms goes back thousands of years: "Normal science, for example, often suppresses fundamental novelties because they are necessarily subversive to its basic commitments." But he points out: "Nevertheless, so long as those commitments retain an element of the arbitrary, the very nature of normal research ensures that novelty shall not be suppressed for very long." (*The Structure of Scientific Revolutions*, p5) The discovery of the cosmic background radiation was just such an "element of the arbitrary".

It is revealing to briefly study one instance of this supposed shifting of the goalposts that Woods pursues through the pages of *Reason in Revolt*. Before the discovery of the cosmic background radiation, theorists realised that if the Big Bang had taken place, there would be a faint afterglow of the original fireball, and were able to calculate the circumstances of the release of this cosmic background radiation. If found, it would be convincing evidence of the Big Bang theory.

Woods describes how the temperature of the cosmic background radiation was differently estimated a number of times before it was discovered. The first attempt at an estimation of the temperature was by George Gamow and Ralph Alpher a quarter of a century before it was observed experimentally.

When the cosmic background radiation was discovered, purely by accident, by two young radio astronomers, Arno Penzias and Robert Wilson, in 1965, it was found to be at a much lower temperature than predicted. They measured a temperature of 3.5 degrees above absolute zero – absolute zero is minus 273 degrees centigrade – very cold indeed! Contemporary Big Bang theorists Robert Dicke and James Peebles had estimated the temperature to be in the region of 35 degrees above absolute zero.

Woods goes so far as to hint that Dicke subsequently made false claims about the accuracy of his original predictions. (p 187) This lack of agreement of original theory and data in relation to temperature is Woods' main argument to discredit the Big Bang origins of the cosmic background radiation. In reality, the early estimates were based on more approximate data, and as new data came in from bigger telescopes, more accurate estimates could be made. When Gamow and Alpher made their original prediction, they used the very approximate value for the rate of expansion of the universe calculated by Hubble in the 1930s.

It is true that there was still a discrepancy between the predicted temperature and the experimental result. But Woods fails to mention any of the other numerous factors of the radiation identified by the radio astronomers Penzias and Wilson, which coincided with the general theoretical conception of the cosmic background radiation model being developed by Big Bang theorists Dicke and Peebles at that time. In technical terms, Dicke and Peebles theorised that the radiation must be black-body radiation, it must be isotropic, unpolarised, have a certain range of temperatures, and a certain range of wavelengths.[1] A further explanation of these concepts would take us a little beyond our remit. Suffice to say that the nature of this radiation was unique and quite specifically determined and identified. All of this meant that when the two teams of scientists, Penzias and Wilson, and Dicke and Peebles, finally learnt about each other's work, they instantly recognised what they had found, despite the temperature discrepancy.

In 1965, the four of them collaborated on publishing their scientific papers announcing the discovery together in the *Astrophysical Journal*. The paper of Penzias and Wilson modestly concentrated on a detailed description of the radiation they had discovered, for which they won the Nobel prize. Dicke and Peebles, (who had intended to set up an experiment to detect this very radiation, until they were beaten to it by Penzias and Wilson) concentrated on just what this discovery meant. The papers are available on the internet (see *Endnote*, p113). Let us take a brief look at the paper, *Cosmic Black-Body Radiation,* by Dicke, Peebles, Roll and Wilkinson. (*Astrophysical Journal* 142: pp414-419, July 1965)

One curiosity the paper reveals is that Dicke and Peebles were working on a cyclical Big Bang model, the type of model of the universe which in the 2002 preface to *Reason in Revolt* Woods falsely says is consistent with dialectical materialism, because it assumes the universe is infinite in time (which we touched on in the chapter, *Engels on materialism, the infinite and cosmology*). This was a common Big Bang model until the time of the discovery of the cosmic background radiation.

Dicke and Peebles worked out the early temperature of the hot dense origins of the universe using the current temperature of the cosmic background radiation newly discovered and determined by Penzias and Wilson. They wrote that during the "highly contracted phase of the universe" a temperature in excess of ten billion degrees "is strongly implied by a present temperature of 3.5° Kelvin for black-body radiation". (*Astrophysical Journal* 142, p416)

This is the temperature that Penzias and Wilson measured. From Penzias and Wilson's measurement, Dicke and Peebles found that there was support for the calculations of the relative abundance of the light elements (mainly hydrogen and helium) made by Hoyle and others, emanating from a hot dense origin of the universe – another of the four pillars of the Big Bang theory, alongside the cosmic background radiation itself. This is compelling evidence for the Big Bang.

A third deduction in their paper relates to the number of atoms per "cubic metre of space" calculation for which Woods gives a figure without recognising its derivation. The authors of the paper somewhat ruefully recognised that, based on the experimental evidence discovered by Penzias and Wilson, the average number of atoms in each cubic metre of space (the density of the universe) was far too low for their own model, the cyclical Big Bang model, to be possible.

The universe appears to be 'open', fated to continue expanding indefinitely, they reluctantly concluded. Their cyclical model, they wrote, required the lower limit of the temperature of the cosmic background radiation to be no lower than thirty degrees above absolute zero, with an upper limit of forty degrees, except under some rather speculative circumstances. At a frigid 3.5 degrees, they wrote, this spelt trouble for their 'closed' universe concept which cycles through big bangs and big crunches.

All these considerations show that Woods' objections to the discrepancies of the temperature of the cosmic background radiation do not in any way invalidate the general nature of the discovery, as he implies. However, the apparent low density (the 'missing matter' problem) of the universe is still a question for major study in cosmology.

Table 5: the situation today

	Motion		Universe		Infinity
	Space	**Time**	**Space**	**Time**	
Aristotle	Absolute Denied the existence of space and time outside the sphere of the universe	Absolute	Finite	Infinite	Denied actual infinite
Galileo	Relative	Relative	Finite (assumed)	Infinite (assumed)	Showed paradoxes of infinite
Newton	Absolute Laws of motion based on relative space & time; assumed absolute space & time real but undetected	Absolute	Infinite	Infinite	God as Infinite
Einstein	Relative	Relative	'Only two things are infinite, the universe and human stupidity, and I'm not sure about the former' (attributed to Einstein). Einstein eventually came to accept a finite universe.		
Today	Relative	Relative	Our universe is finite in time and space. Beyond our universe nothing is known.	In general, scientists regard infinities which arise in calculations as indicating an error.	

There is no headlong rush to mysticism in these four pillars of the Big Bang theory, which adhere entirely to the material evidence, as opposed to the occult of Newton's universal gravitation. In fact, it is Woods who abandons a materialist approach in order to explain the origins of this supposed mysticism. He argues that subjective idealism, Einstein's supposed "philosophical mistake", has had the most "harmful influence upon modern science". (p167) And he cites the autobiography of the virulently anti-Marxist philosopher Karl Popper to back him up. According to Popper, Einstein confided his "mistake" to him, Woods informs us. Woods takes this as good coin:

"All the nonsense about "the observer" as a determining factor was not an essential part of the theory, but merely the reflection of a philosophical mistake, as Einstein frankly confirmed." (p167)

What Woods terms "nonsense" is in fact a straw man resurrected by him based on past philosophical misinterpretations of Einstein. It is astonishing to see Woods quoting Popper uncritically. Popper's works and followers are saturated with an active hostility to dialectics and Marxism. Popper's works are harmful to science and the philosophy of science.

It is not a materialist approach to attribute to a "philosophical mistake" the emergence of a supposed "mysticism" more rampant than at any other time in the history of science. This appears to be more of an idealist approach: to seek to explain developments in human society primarily through the development or influence of philosophical ideas, mistaken or otherwise, rather than to look for their material basis.

Creation of matter

Woods often argues against the coming into being of our universe in the following way:

"From the standpoint of dialectical materialism, it is arrant nonsense to talk about the 'beginning of time' or the 'creation of matter'. Time, space, and motion are the mode of existence of matter, which can neither be created nor destroyed." (p198-9)

Woods bases his argument essentially on the law of the conservation of mass and energy, which basically says that the total amount of mass and energy of a system must be conserved. He says, "there is one law which knows no exception in nature – the law of the conservation of energy". (p108)

Let us disregard for a moment that some scientists suspect there are small breaches in this law at the quantum level over very short periods of time. The law of conservation of mass and energy appears to apply generally within the confines of our universe, the physics of our four dimensional space-time. But suppose that there is a substratum which underpins space-time, perhaps a world from which our four dimensional space-time is an emergent property, the tip of an iceberg, a qualitative change in special circumstances. Suppose that in other circumstances quite a different configuration of physics emerges from this primeval flux? This is, of course, speculative.

But let's look at the matter historically. Hermann Helmholtz is often considered to be the first to formulate a law of conservation of force in 1847, although others, including Descartes, had proposed similar theories. He later said: "If we are fully acquainted with a natural law, we must also demand that it should operate without exception." Engels, who quotes

Helmholtz here (*Dialectics of Nature*, pp108-9), ridicules the fact that Helmholtz goes on to admit that we "objectivise laws which in the first place embrace only a limited series of natural processes, the conditions for which are still rather complicated". In other words, Engels explains, Helmholtz admits that while scientists may demand that a law is applicable without exception in nature they are often far from understanding it, let alone proving its eternal validity. Historically, it can be seen that our understanding of physical laws is contingent on our understanding of physical processes, and that laws come into being and pass away in revolutions in physics which render the old laws inapplicable. Thus, in the nineteenth century, the laws of conservation of energy, or more strictly of mass-energy, replaced the law of conservation of '*vis viva*' or 'living force' proposed by Leibniz around the period 1676-89.

It may be objected that the conservation of mass and energy is common sense – things do not pop up out of nowhere. This appears to be the way questions are often treated in *Reason in Revolt*: statements are made that, it is assumed, simply require no justification, no evidence, as if one should rely on common sense. But we are not talking about our everyday experience, but the extreme limits of nature and our scientific knowledge.

The second problem with Woods' approach is much simpler: it simply does not follow from the law of conservation of mass and energy that matter and energy cannot be created or destroyed, only that the total mass and energy of a system must be conserved.

In other words, the law of conservation of mass and energy does not contradict the dialectic of coming into being and passing away, whether at the subatomic, quantum level, or at the cosmic level, so long as energy and mass are conserved overall. It is speculated that our universe is comprised of opposites so that, for instance, all the mass and energy of the universe is exactly equal to its opposite, gravity, so that they cancel out. In this way, it is speculated, the law of conservation of mass and energy was not broken when all the matter and energy of our universe emerged in the Big Bang, along with its negation, gravity.

Woods ascribes to matter and energy indestructible and uncreated properties, which he wrongly believes follows from the law of the conservation of energy. Interestingly, Engels says this on the question of the law of conservation of energy:

"*Whereas only ten years ago the great basic law of motion, then recently discovered, was as yet conceived merely as a law of the conservation of energy, as the mere expression of the indestructibility and uncreatability of motion, that is, merely in its quantitative aspect, this narrow negative conception is being more and more supplanted by the positive idea of the transformation of energy, in which for the first time the qualitative content of the process comes into its own, and the last vestige of an extramundane creator [e.g. Newton's god] is obliterated.*

1885 Preface, *Anti-Dühring*, p18

In our view, Engels would have embraced the ideas of Einstein, of the transformation of mass into energy and vice versa. Engels stressed the discoveries of the transformation of different forms of energy – heat, light, mechanical motion. He was thrilled at the discovery of the conservation of energy only because of its recognition of these transformations. The conservation, the indestructibility and uncreatability of motion, Engels sees as a narrow negative conception, "the last vestige of an extramundane creator", which is being "supplanted" by concepts of the transformation of energy.

Nineteenth century mechanical conceptions were found to be inadequate by the beginning of the twentieth century. Quantum mechanics, one of the most successful of modern scientific theories, shows that if a particle with positive energy comes into being out of nothing (perhaps from some as yet unidentified substratum), a particle with negative energy also comes into being. Matter and energy are thus conserved while at the same time the narrow negative conception of the conservation of mass and energy is lost. No wonder, then, that physicists were not completely unprepared for a rather larger version of this quantum creation and destruction of matter in the Big Bang, only given that there was sufficient evidence, a smoking gun, which was provided by the cosmic background radiation.

Woods, on the other hand, precisely stresses the narrow, negative conception of merely the conservation of energy and mass, in order to justify his undialectical concept of an infinite universe, which is beyond material proof.

Woods suggests that dialectical materialism has a special privileged way of determining scientific questions in advance of any evidence. In truth, Woods is merely regurgitating the efforts of nineteenth century physics that were summed up in the first law of thermodynamics – the conservation of energy – and giving it his endorsement.

1   Radiation takes the form of 'black-body radiation' if a primordial fireball like the Big Bang radiated it before there was any other radiation in existence. Stars radiate into almost empty space, and emit almost perfect black body radiation as far as

astronomy is concerned. But the detected cosmic background radiation is much closer to a perfect black body, immediately suggesting a more primordial origin. Crudely speaking, black-body radiation is radiation which is characteristic of the radiating system only, that is, it shows no indication of having any radiation incident upon it, as it were, from other radiating bodies.

The dialectic of the unity and interpenetration of opposites in science

As briefly mentioned earlier, Woods follows Eric Lerner's general approach to the Big Bang. Lerner, adopting a popular style, argues that the Big Bang theory is full of holes. This is misleading. When pressed, Lerner makes clear he rejects the Big Bang theory because one or more of its predictions have from time to time failed – such as the original calculations of the temperature of the cosmic background radiation mentioned above.

Science according to Karl Popper

Lerner takes the position that: "When a theory makes clear predictions which are contradicted by observation it is falsified and has to be rejected." (http://www.physicsforums.com/showthread.php?t=89106&page=2) What Lerner expresses here is the well-known philosophy of the anti-Marxist, anti-dialectician Karl Popper. In broad terms, Popper said that if a single observation falsifies a scientific theory, the theory is wrong, and must be abandoned. He argued that if a science relies on theories that do not admit of falsification, or if a science simply modifies its claims to circumvent falsification, it can no longer be thought of as a science, but at best is no more than a "metaphysical research programme", and at worst is no different to mysticism, like astrology.

In its original and popular form, Popper's mode of falsification may be conceived in terms of a single experimental result, which is capable of producing data that can falsify the scientific theory under investigation. This idea has entered into our common sense notions of science, but is an inadequate and misleading depiction of the methodology of science.

While there are many celebrated examples of falsification – such as the Michelson and Morley null result which failed to prove the existence of the aether discussed above – closer historical examination of such examples shows that this oversimplifies the situation. In the case of the Michelson and Morley experiment, there were serious conceptual problems with the very idea of the aether. There were related problems of how James Clerk Maxwell's theory of electromagnetism was linked to the physics of light. There was a period of crisis in physics. There were a whole series of experiments, each of increasing accuracy and ingenuity, before and after the celebrated Michelson and Morley experiment, and yet scientists were at a loss as to what exactly was wrong. It was the combined weight of these failures, together with the emergence of Einstein's theory of relativity, which finally overthrew the old Newtonian physics and the aether theory together.

Popper came to recognise that his original conception was inadequate, and modified his theory in various ways to circumvent criticism. Lerner uses the "naïve falsification" popularly associated with Popper's theory to dismiss the current Big Bang theory, while some have used Popper's theory to suggest that cosmology itself is not a science, arguing that it cannot, by its very nature, be falsified in the way Popper conceived.

But this only demonstrates that Popper's theory of falsification was too narrow. In every field, including physics and especially cosmology, science advances on a broad front and requires evaluation, comparison and judgement of a wide range of evidence (often apparently conflicting) over time. For this reason, it is inappropriate to cast science into the mould of simple true/false laboratory tests. This is most clear in the sciences that are far removed from the experimental laboratory, such as the sciences which study evolution, archaeology, palaeontology, and so forth, but it applies in cosmology too.

Popper falsely argues that Marxism is not based on a scientific method since, he asserts, it has shown itself to be not falsifiable. Events, Popper argues, have provided evidence of the falseness of Marxism as a theory, and yet it has refused to die. Marxists argue that Popper and his followers display a profound lack of understanding of Marxist theory, if not a determined opposition to it. Popper famously concluded at one point that, according to his criterion, Darwinian evolution is not science. This is essentially because Darwinian evolution, a little like Marxism, does not generally avail itself of simple laboratory tests.

Yet the truth is that no science reduces itself to the simple criterion Popper proposes, as the example of the temperature of the cosmic background radiation in the previous chapter, *The Big Bang and mysticism in science*, shows.

Vulgar materialism and positivism

Popper's theory of falsification fails its own test – it cannot be falsified. The theory is problematic since the falsifying observations themselves may turn out to be false. But these are merely technical objections. The truth is that complex phenomena such as scientific theories evolve in time, and any modern science is a complex result of historical development. By contrast, it is in the nature of what is termed 'positivist' philosophy to attempt to reduce all things to simple facts, the atomic components, as it were, that make up the whole, rather than approaching things in a holistic manner. Although he refused the title, Popper was correctly seen as the representative of modern positivism in Britain. In their day Hegel and Marx were both hostile to all varieties of atomistic positivism, from the ancient Greek atomists to the positivists of their day.

Dialectics has always opposed this simplistic approach. The evaluation of scientific theories requires a comparative analysis of a wide range of observation and theories – all facets of the phenomenon. By comparison, Popper's approach is reductionist: it tends to take the falsifying evidence in isolation (as Woods does in the cosmic background radiation temperature discrepancy) rather than examining the whole in its historical develop-ment. Some of the most prominent scientists have attested to the inadequacies of Popper's approach, such as Stephen Hawking in *A Brief History of Time*, and Roger Penrose in *The Road to Reality: A Complete Guide to the Laws of the Universe*, a thousand-page book aimed at giving a comprehensive guide to the laws of physics, published in 2004. Penrose says Popper's method is "too stringent a criterion, and definitely too idealis-tic a view of science in this modern world of 'Big science'." (*The Road to Reality*, p1,020)

Unfortunately, however, many scientists still pay lip service to Popper's basic contention, even if in their daily practice they do not apply his method. Some, like the physicist Lee Smolin, appear to have an inconsis-tent or pragmatic outlook. Smolin demands that a theory is not only falsifi-able, but also "confirmable" – something Popper denies is possible. Further, when Smolin discusses *What is Science?* he embraces the philosophy of Paul Feyerabend, a fierce critic of Popper. (Smolin, *The Trouble with Physics*, pxiii and p290)

Of course, any materialist, considering the Big Bang theory, would rightly object to the notion that something can come from nothing. But as we have said before, science assumes a substratum. Science continually uncovers as yet unknown physical processes. If something appears to spring from nothing, it indicates that there are limits to our scientific understanding, an understanding that does not encompass all aspects of reality. Marxists cannot take the crude approach exemplified by *Reason in Revolt*.

In fact, sometimes Woods takes a very crude approach to science: "In the last analysis, all human existence and activity is based on the laws of the motion of atoms." (p60) This is not true in any sense, let alone in the last analysis. In the very simplest sense it omits gravity, photons of light and so forth. But it is an indication of the eclectic method of Woods that he then immediately proceeds to assert the opposite: "Nobody in their right mind would seek to explain the complex movements in human society in terms of atomic forces." (p60) What does he mean then by "in the last analysis"? Cells, animals, species, consciousness, social organisation – most complex things cannot be reduced to the laws of the motion of atoms, "in the last analysis".

Later, Woods applauds the ancient Greek atomists "who visualised the universe as being composed of only two things – the 'atoms' and the 'void'. In essence, this view of the universe is correct." (p145) It is not true in essence or in any other sense. It is the crudest, most ancient expression of the philosophy of positivism of which Popper is a descendent – the modern school properly began with Auguste Comte in the early nineteenth century, and with which outlook *Reason in Revolt* is flawed. This time Woods does not stop to contradict himself, but leaves this crude reductionist position to stand. Marx and Engels rejected the philosophy of Comte and those who took up a similar position later in the century.

Dialectics and science

In any case, from a dialectical point of view, everything that changes has within it an interpenetration of opposites, as Engels puts it in *Dialectics of Nature*. This dialectic applies in the field of science, and certainly brings us nearer to a Marxist understanding of the nature of scientific theories. Some opposing, contradictory data is likely to be unaccounted for by any scientific model in any field, especially the more ambitious models.

In the "great dialectic between theory and data", as the palaeontologist Stephen Jay Gould called it, good scientific modelling attempts to find common ground in a riot of data. The Big Bang theory famously confronts a number of contradictions, the most important of which is how it came into being out of nothing. We have attempted to show that modern science is no stranger to the dialectic of coming into being, even if it does not consciously recognise this dialectic. But none of these contradictions yet seriously challenge the validity of the four pillars of experimental data that confirm the Big Bang theory. Instead, the contradictions lead to further developments and new conceptualisations of the universe and its contents, further experiments and discoveries.

As well as contradictions confronting scientific models themselves, there are also opposing political and social pressures on scientists to interpret their data in various ways. Take global warming. Enormous political pressures were placed by various elements of the ruling elite, particularly within George W Bush's regime in the USA, on those scientists who defended the theory of global warming against the theory's opponents, which included some of the large, powerful sections of the capitalist class that Bush represents, like major oil companies. This may now be beginning to change.

Yet the vast majority of genuine researchers in the field of global warming were prepared to oppose these political pressures. Why is this? There are divisions within the ruling class on the question of the environment, since some corporations fear a backlash arising from the failures of big business-led governments to counter global warming, among other concerns. This same pressure is no doubt felt within the scientific community, as well as being fed by it. Woods treats the scientific establishment as if it is monolithic, but it too suffers from the interpenetration of opposites. Scientific teams of researchers, at any rate, are in many cases skilled workers themselves, even if the grants, bursaries and investment in science are coming more and more under the thumb of the capitalist class at the present time.

In fact, contradictions in and between scientific theories and their data abound within science, as any practising scientist knows. We have shown how Newton was aware of contradictions in his own model of the universe, such as the problem of the collapse of the universe under its own gravity. There will always be data that is untamed, alternative interpretations, contradictory material. Some contradictions indicate the path down which a more advanced theory may one day be found, leading at a certain point to a revolutionary overturn of the old paradigm and the establishment of a new paradigm, which then largely dictates the outlook and direction of scientific research and its theoretical development over a whole period of time, as the philosopher Thomas Kuhn argued in *The Structure of Scientific Revolutions* in 1962. Thus the Newtonian paradigm of space and time was overthrown two centuries later by Einstein's space-time paradigm and the Big Bang theory, resolving contradictions that had existed since Newton's day. We cannot discuss the merits of Kuhn's work here, but Kuhn is certainly right when he points out that a paradigm "need not, and in fact never does, explain all the facts with which it can be confronted". (*The Structure of Scientific Revolutions*, p18)

Woods rather disdainfully writes that Kuhn's philosophy of science "can be accepted as true" (p380), although, in typical eclectic fashion, in the preceding paragraphs he embraces some of the very ideas Kuhn was successfully refuting. Woods can hardly argue that Kuhn's approach, which has elements of a dialectical outlook, informs Woods' own approach to science in *Reason in Revolt*, since the opposite is true. There is no question that the accumulation of material evidence is critical to the advancement of science. But Woods' approach is too simplistic.

Contradictions found in scientific theories, such as the Big Bang theory, might indicate the dying embers of an old, negated paradigm, or aspects of it preserved but represented in unrevised methods and outmoded supporting theories, outdated instruments operating at the far limits of their range, or techniques that are still far from adequate.

Hegel explains that in the course of human development the negation of old ideas (or paradigms) does not simply mean that human history is a meaningless process of endless errors. Something is always preserved in the course of the negation. Now this something might be a positive or a negative hangover (or a mixture of both), but it indicates, as Kuhn hastened to emphasise after the publication of *The Structure of Scientific Revolutions*, that there is a continuing development of a greater understanding of the cosmos, in contrast to those philosophers who deny any progress at all. There seems to be insufficient recognition of the nature of this dialectical process of new ideas coming into being in *Reason in Revolt*.

In the collection of essays, *It Ain't Necessarily So*, the evolutionary biologist and social commentator, Richard Lewontin, puts it like this, beginning with an oblique reference to the same revolution that inspired Hegel:

"As in politics, so in science, a genuine revolution is not an event but a process. A manifesto may be published, a reigning head may drop into a basket, but the accumulated contradictions of the past do not disappear in an instant. Nor do the supporters of the ancien régime. The new view of nature does indeed resolve many of the old problems, but it creates new ones of its own, new contradictions that are different from, but not necessarily any less deep than, the old. And waiting, just across the border, are intellectual somocistas, saying, "I told you so. What did you expect?" trying to convince us that the old way of looking at nature was correct after all. Of course, the old view of nature can never return, but rather new revolutions displace old ones."

Darwin's Revolution, New York Review of Books, 16 June 1983.
(The Somocistas were reactionary landlord supporters of the US backed
Nicaraguan dictator Somoza prior to the 1979 revolution).

Only a complete theory would consistently explain everything – and no theory is ever complete because observations constantly reveal new phenomena that require new, higher levels of theoretical understanding. Woods, however, rejects the entire body of the modern science of cosmology, calling it creationism: "The Big Bang theory is really a creation myth," complete with "its inseparable companion, the day of Final Judgement (the 'Big Crunch')." (p183) This accusation of a creation myth, made by Hoyle (who died in 2001), and other opponents of the Big Bang theory – at least until the discovery of the cosmic background radiation forty years ago – is regarded by scientists as simply casting aspersions. On its own it is not a scientific refutation. If Woods wishes to criticise the Big Bang, he must do so by thoroughly examining – in an informed and balanced way – the experimental evidence.

Idealist approach

In the chapter, *The Theory of Knowledge*, Woods elucidates the main reason why he feels there is mysticism in science: "… there has been no adequate philosophy which could help to point science in the right direction. The philosophy of science is in a mess." (p381)

This is Woods' justification for writing a book on a subject that he knows very little about: he is the philosopher bringing dialectics to the misguided or ignorant scientist. *Reason in Revolt* attempts to use philosophical reason to revolt against modern science, calling on the assistance of dialectics. As we have seen, Woods' acquaintance with philosophy also appears to be sketchy.

Woods reiterates that "Einstein was partly responsible" for the supposed tendency to mysticism in science. (p381) Once again we must insist that this is not a materialist approach. It is not helped by a complaint of "prejudice against dialectics". (p385) However true that may be, and however much it may hinder the rapid development of science, it is still no material barrier which could send science backwards, let alone so far back that at "no time in the history of science has mysticism been so rampant as now". (p384)

As long ago as 1885, Engels concluded that "natural science has now advanced so far that it can no longer escape dialectical generalisation".

Twentieth century scientific theory, in particular quantum mechanics, in many ways soon proved this to be the case. Engels merely notes that the scientist can arrive at these generalisations "more easily if one approaches the dialectical character of these facts equipped with an understanding of the laws of dialectical thought." (1885 preface to *Anti-Dühring*, pp19-20)

On the whole, however, Woods puts the causes of the supposed descent into mysticism of science down to philosophical mistakes. This is a very one-sided approach that has fallen into idealism. Hegel, the consummate idealist, would – indeed did – take the same position. Science, he said, was a "kind of witches' circle in which... phenomena and phantoms run riot in indiscriminate company and enjoy equal rank with one another." (*Science of Logic*, p461) Hegel was an idealist philosopher. Marx and Engels broke from that view.

So should Marxists defend the Big Bang theory? Such a question would indicate a wrong approach to Marxist dialectics. We have tried to show that Marxism does not supply an a priori means of determining correct scientific theories – it cannot dictate by means of materialist dialectics which scientific theory is verifiable and which is not.

In general terms only a genuinely socialist society could re-establish workers' confidence in the results of modern science, once science is no longer subject to the malign influence of big business agendas. In 1926, Trotsky wrote:

> "*Although class interests have introduced and are still introducing false tendencies even into natural science, nevertheless this falsification process is restricted by the limits beyond which it begins directly to prevent the progress of technology.*"
>
> *Problems of Everyday Life*, p287

This is still true today. But scientific thought will only demonstrate truly "vast possibilities" once it is

> "*... so to speak, nationalised, emancipated from the internecine wars of private property, no longer required to lend itself to bribery of individual proprietors, but intended to serve the economic development of the nation as a whole.*"
>
> *Problems of Everyday Life*, p274

Only then could we perhaps envisage the development of the social and political toolkit of Marxism into one which embraces and encourages independent scientific development (without any *a priori* judgements). Then, instead of perhaps in their ones and twos today, scientists as a body will be able to consciously apply dialectical considerations as an aid to their work.

But Trotsky issued the following warning:

"*Whenever any Marxist attempted to transmute the theory of Marx into a universal master key and ignore all other spheres of learning, Vladimir Ilyich [Lenin] would rebuke him with the expressive phrase 'Komchvanstvo' ('communist swagger').*"

Problems of Everyday Life, p274

Dialectics and the universe

Science has demonstrated the dialectics of the universe. Some ten to twenty billion years ago, so far as is most broadly accepted by science today, there was a sudden catastrophic dialectical transformation, and the universe we know came into existence – from what cause we do not know. Time and space are bound up with matter and energy, and are not exempt from the dialectics of nature. Time has not been ticking eternally, exempt from the transformations of quantity into quality first discovered by the ancient philosophers of Ionia, and which in modern times helped form the Marxist understanding of processes here on earth.

Woods supposes that time is exempt from this dialectical transformation. In arguing for an infinite universe, Woods steps from the path of materialism and science, and onto a path towards what Hegel termed 'metaphysics'. By metaphysics here we mean both a non-dialectical approach and an attempt to base a philosophy on a realm beyond the world of experience. The science of the Big Bang presents both a more material and a more dialectical view of the universe than that of *Reason in Revolt*. Woods dismisses the scientific evidence of the Big Bang without a proper consideration of that evidence. Is this dialectical materialism? Surely it is the opposite.

Some of the modern theories of the cosmos contain a rediscovery (not for the first time) by science of the dialectics of nature. The theory of cosmological phase changes or transitions helped scientists make definite predictions that have been experimentally proved, as Greene explains. He says "cosmological phase transitions have proven so potent" that many scientists feel that the concept of phase transitions will contribute to a unified theory of the cosmos. (*The Fabric of the Cosmos*, p268) They are used in theories of how the early universe developed. Phase transitions are an example of the dialectic of the transformation of quantity into quality and vice versa.

One thing is certain: an infinite universe can never be tested for or detected by a telescope, or any other instrument. The origin of the concept of an infinite universe is not to be found in nature but in the mind. It is an idea, and to argue that our universe is infinite in time and space in the twenty-first century is a move backwards to the epoch of the origins of Newtonian physics, and towards a philosophy of idealism.

Conclusion

At the beginning of this review, we suggested that Woods has a less than rounded-out grasp of science. He does not understand how water boils. He does not recognise Newton's first law of motion, attributing it to Einstein's relativity, and then attempts to discredit it. Had he chosen any other of Newton's laws to discredit, he might have been correct, if only by chance, but he fell upon the one Newtonian law which remains fundamental to physics. Woods attempts to defend the Newtonian universe, yet no more recognises the fact than he does Newton's laws.

But it was not Woods' scientific pretensions that led us to review *Reason in Revolt*. Woods claimed, in his obituary to Ted Grant, that *Reason in Revolt* defends the fundamentals of Marxism. We strongly object. Woods supposes that dialectical materialism takes as axiomatic the Newtonian universe. He misrepresents 2,500 years of science and philosophy to support this mistake. He fails to grasp the dialectic between theory and experiment, and has little understanding of scientific method.

He calls on Hegel for support. Whereas Marx and Engels took Hegel's dialectical idealism and stood it on its feet, creating what became known as dialectical materialism, Woods spins it around to get metaphysical idealism. He reverses Hegel's rejection of the spurious infinite universe, embracing this undialectical ideal in the name of Marxism. Marx and Engels abandoned Hegel's system and kept his dialectical method. Woods defends Newtonian absolute space and time, which Hegel incorporates into his Absolute Idea, and abandons Hegel's dialectical method which contradicts it.

Woods misrepresents both Hegel and Engels. Engels explicitly praised Kant's insight into the coming into being of our universe, yet Woods makes no mention of it. He attempts to turn Engels' understanding of science into a timeless dogma, and ignores Engels' dialectical method, which points clearly to the conclusion that our universe must have come into being and will pass away.

We have attempted to present an alternative to the reader, by discussing the historical development of ideas about the universe, which led eventually to the astounding and counter-intuitive theories of today: Einstein's relativity, quantum mechanics, and the Big Bang. Marxism does not have the tools to evaluate these sciences independently of a full comprehension of the scientific evidence, incomplete as it always will be, purely on the strength of its philosophical method. Yet Woods supposes that dialectical materialism has some *a priori* ability to judge the correctness of a science, expressing an affinity for Popper, who thought that his method of falsification could do the same.

We have pointed to a more dialectical understanding of the nature of science, and briefly outlined the undoubtedly dialectical elements in modern scientific theories about the universe. Science will continue to develop and change, as will our understanding of the universe. In the last century, however, we have witnessed several remarkable revolutions in science, overturning centuries-old paradigms. Some may find them shocking and disturbing – just as shocking no doubt, as the ancient Ionians found the philosophy of Anaximander, who two-and-a-half millennia ago said the world had come into existence in a ball of fire and would eventually pass away. But these revolutions, which have opened such vast, unexplored horizons – even of universes beyond our universe – must not tempt us into false notions of the infinite.

End note

The two classic papers on cosmic background radiation are:

A Measurement of Excess Antenna Temperature at 4080 Mc/s

A.A. Penzias & R.W. Wilson

Astrophysical Journal 142: 419-421, July 1965

http://adsabs.harvard.edu/cgi-bin/nph-bib_query?bibcode=1965ApJ...142..419

P&db_key=AST&high=3cf96e067109101

Cosmic Black-Body Radiation

R.H. Dicke et al.

Astrophysical Journal 142: 414-419, July, 1965

http://adsabs.harvard.edu/cgi-bin/nph-bib_query?bibcode=1965ApJ...142..414

D&db_key=AST&high=3cf96e067109368

Bibliography

Where page numbers are given in the text, they refer to the pages in the particular editions of the publications listed here:

Anaximander: http://www.iep.utm.edu/a/anaximan.htm

Aristotle, *Physics*, http://classics.mit.edu/Aristotle/physics.html

Aristotle, *On the Heavens*, http://classics.mit.edu/Aristotle/heavens.html

Barrow, John D., *The Infinite Book*, Vintage, 2005

Big Bang: The four pillars of the Hot Big Bang model are discussed at the Cambridge university Department of Applied Mathematics and Theoretical Physics: 'A Brief History of Observational Cosmology' at: http://www.damtp.cam.ac.uk/user/gr/public/bb_home.html

Calder, Nigel, *Einstein's Universe, the layman's guide*, Penguin/Pelican 1998

Copernicus, Nicolaus, *On the revolutions of Heavenly Spheres*, in *On the Shoulders of Giants* edited by Stephen Hawking, Penguin, 2002.

Dicke, R.H. et al., *Cosmic Black-Body Radiation*, Astrophysical Journal 142: 414-419, July, 1965

Einstein, Albert, *Relativity*, Methuen, 1960

Einstein, *On the electrodynamics of moving bodies* (paper on special relativity, 1905), *The Foundation of the general theory of relativity*, (1916) and *Cosmological considerations on the general theory of relativity*, (1917) are all in *On the Shoulders of Giants* edited by Stephen Hawking, Penguin, 2002.

Engels, Frederich, *Anti-Dühring*, Progress Publishers, Moscow, 1969
Engels, Frederich, *Dialectics of Nature*, Moscow 1954,
    Lawrence and Wishart, 1955
Engels, Frederich, *Ludwig Feuerbach and the Outcome of Classical German
    Philosophy*, *Marx and Engels Selected works* in one volume
Engels, *Socialism, Utopian and Scientific*, *Marx and Engels Selected
    works* in one volume.
Galileo, *Dialogues Concerning Two Sciences* is in print complete in a new
    collection, *On the Shoulders of Giants* edited by Stephen Hawking,
    Penguin, 2002.
Galileo, *Dialogue Concerning the Two Chief World Systems*. The relevant
    excerpt is currently at http://en.wikipedia.org/wiki/Galileo's_ship
Gamow, George, *Mr Tompkins* in paperback, Cambridge University Press, 1965
Gleick, James, *Issac Newton*, Fourth Estate, 2003
Gould, Stephen Jay, *Eight Little Piggies*, Penguin, 1993
Gott, J. Richard, *Time travel in Einstein's universe*, Phoenix, 2002
Greene, Brian, *The Elegant Universe*, Vintage, 2000
Greene, Brian, *The Fabric of the Cosmos,* Penguin, 2005
Gribbin, John, *In search of the Big Bang, the life and death of the universe,*
    Penguin, 1998
Hawking, Stephen W., *A Brief History of Time,* Bantam Press, 1989
Hegel, GWF, Encyclopaedia see: http://www.marxists.org/reference/
    archive/hegel/works/ol/encycind.htm
Hegel, GWF, *Science of Logic*, Humanity Books/ Prometheus Books, 1998.
    The *Science of Logic* is on the internet at http://www.marxists.org/reference/
    archive/hegel/works/hl/. A google search on a phrase of Hegel's quoted
    here, enclosed in double quotes, will often take you directly to the webpage,
    where a search of the page will take you to the passage in question.
Hoffmann, Banesh, *Einstein*, Granada / Paladin, 1982
Hoyle, Fred, *Frontiers of astronomy*, Signet, 1963
Janiak, A. (ed.), 2004, *Newton: Philosophical Writings*, Cambridge:
    Cambridge University Press.

Kant, *Prolegomena to any Future Metaphysic that can Present itself as a Science*,
  http://www.earlymoderntexts.com/pdf/kantprol.pdf
Khun, Thomas S, *The structure of scientific revolutions*,
  University of Chicago Press, 3rd edition, 1996
Lenin, *Conspectus of Hegel's Book, The Science of Logic*, in his *Collected Works*,
  Progress Publishers, Moscow, 1965, Volume 38, p.85-242
Lewontin, Richard, *It Ain't Necessarily So*,
Marx and Engels, *Selected Works* in one volume, Lawrence and Wishart, 1968
Newton, Issac, *Principia*, is in print complete in a new collection,
  On the Shoulders of Giants edited by Stephen Hawking, Penguin, 2002.
Newton, Issac: See the *Stanford Encyclopaedia of Philosophy* for a discussion
  on Newton's Views on Space, Time, and Motion:
  http://plato.stanford.edu/entries/newton-stm/
Novack, George, *The Origins of Materialism*, Merit/Pathfinder Press, 1971
Penrose, Roger *The Road to Reality: A Complete Guide to the Laws
  of the Universe*, Vintage, 2004
Penzias, A.A. & R.W. Wilson, *A Measurement of Excess Antenna Temperature at
  4080 Mc/s*, Astrophysical Journal 142: 419-421, July 1965
Plekhanov, Georgi, *The development of the monist view of history*, Moscow, 1956
Rees, Martin, *Before the beginning, Our Universe and others*, Touchstone, 1998
Singh, Simon, *Big Bang*, Harper Perennial, 2005. I recommend this book
  as an introduction to the subject.
Smolin, *The Trouble with Physics*, Allen Lane / Penguin (Hardback edition) 2007
Trotsky, Leon, Problems of Everyday Life, Pathfinder Press, 1994
Woods, Alan, and Ted Grant, *Reason in Revolt*, Wellred publications, London,
  1995 (Alan Woods should not be confused with Allen W. Wood, who
  also writes on Karl Marx, and is a Professor of Philosophy
  at Stanford University, USA)

socialist publications

All of the books listed below are available from Socialist Books. To order further copies of this publication or any from either the list or the many other publications published by Socialist Books contact us at:

Socialist Books, PO Box 24697, London E11 1YD
telephone: 020 8988 8789 or email: socialistbooks@socialistparty.org.uk
or online at the socialist books **website: www.socialistbooks.co.uk**

recent titles available from socialist publications

- **Marxism in Today's World: Answers on War, Capitalism and the Environment**
  by Peter Taaffe
  Published November 2006. 128 pages paperback
  This book is the result of a discussion with Italian Marxist, Yurii Colombo, it tackles head on vital contemporary issues: war, including the Lebanese conflict, the future of Israel/Palestine, the environment, China and its future, economic prospects for world capitalism and many more controversial issues. This book provides an invaluable Marxist analysis.
  Price £7.50

- **1926 General Strike: Workers Taste Power**
  by Peter Taaffe
  Published May 2006. 192 pages paperback
  Written to commemorate the eightieth anniversary of the 1926 General Strike in Britain and, more importantly, to draw the lessons from this movement.
  Price £7.50

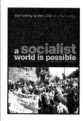

- **A Socialist World is Possible: The History of the CWI**
  by Peter Taaffe
  Published August 2004. 96 pages paperback
  An account and celebration of the activity and contribution of the Committee for a Workers International (CWI) on the 30 Anniversary of its founding, showing how the role and influence of the organisation has developed and change -, in some regions of the world quite dramatically - from its humble origins.
  Price £5.00

other titles available
from socialist publications

- **Pamphlet: 1917: the year that changed the world** by Hannah Sell & Peter Taaffe
  Published October 2007. 32 pages paperback
  Looking at the lessons to be learned from the October Revolution Price £3.00
- **Pamphlet: Planning Green Growth: A Socialist Contribution to the Debate
  on Environmental Sustainability** by Pete Dickenson
  Published January 2003. 32 pages paperback
  *Analysing the causes and scope of environmental destruction and asking the
  question - what is the way forward?* Price £3.00
- **Global Warning: Socialism and the Environment** by Martin Cock & Bill Hopwood
  Published September 1996. 188 pages paperback
  *Esssential reading both for environmentalists who want a better understanding of
  the socialist viewpoint and socialist activists.* Price £6.95
- **Empire Defeated - Vietnam War: The Lessons for Today** by Peter Taaffe
  Published February 2004. 128 pages paperback
  *A history of the Vietnam War drawing out the lessons to be learnt from this conflict,
  especially in the aftermath of the Iraq war.* Price £6.00
- **Pamphlet: Join the Campaign for a New Workers' Party** by The Socialist Party
  Published February 2006. 36 pages paperback
  *A brief explanation of why the Socialist Party has initiated the Campaign for a New
  Workers' Party.* Price £1.00
- **A Civil War without Guns:**
  20 Years On: the lessons of the 1984-85 Miners' Strike by Ken Smith
  Published May 2004. 128 pages paperback
  A balance sheet of this important struggle. Price £5.00
- **Socialism in the 21st Century:**
  The Way Forward for Anti-Capitalism by Hannah Sell.
  Published August 2002. New Updated Edition February 2006. 96 pages paperback
  An essential read for all anti-capitalists, trade union activists and socialists. Price £5.00
- **Che Guevara: Symbol of Struggle** by Tony Saunois.
  Published September 2005. 96 pages paperback
  An appraisal of the life and role of Che Guevara as a revolutionary. Price £5.00
- **Cuba: Socialism and Democracy:**
  Debates on the Revolution and Cuba Today by Peter Taaffe.
  Published 2000. 128 pages paperback
  Defence of the Socialist Party's analysis of the Cuban revolution. Price £5.00
- **The Rise of Militant: Militant's 30 years** by Peter Taaffe.
  Published 1995. 570 pages paperback
  *Story of Militant, forerunner of the Socialist Party (English and Welsh section
  of the CWI), from its birth.* Price £10.99
- **Liverpool - A City that Dared to Fight** by Tony Mulhearn & Peter Taaffe.
  Published 1988, 500 pages paperback
  The *Militant led Liverpool city council's battle against the Thatcher government
  1983-1997.* Price £7.95

the socialist party

join us | I would like to find out more about / join the Socialist Party ❏

Name

Address

Postcode

Tel No | Email

Trade Union (if applicable)

If you are interested in finding out more about the Socialist Party
or our publications simply fill in this form and return to:
Socialist Party, PO Box 24697, London E11 1YD
email: join@socialistparty.org.uk tel: 020 8988 8767
website: **www.socialistparty.org.uk**

the socialist

weekly paper of the Socialist Party

Get your copy of **the socialist** delivered regularly by
subscribing. There is a special introductory offer of 10
issues for only £6.00.

subscription rates:
● 12 issues: £9.00
● 6 months: £18.00
● 1 year: £36.00

You can telephone for either a direct debit form or
pay by credit card on: **020 8988 8796**
the address to contact about subscriptions and
international rates is: **Socialist Party -
Subscriptions, PO Box 24697, London E11 1YD**